The AuDHD Parent Burnout Reset

A Practical Recovery Guide for Autistic and ADHD Parents Exhausted by Demand-Avoidant Parenting

Ruth Margie Holmes

The AuDHD Family Series, Book 2

The content of this book is intended for informational and educational purposes only and does not constitute medical, psychological, psychiatric, or therapeutic advice. Nothing in this publication should be interpreted as a diagnosis, a clinical assessment, or a substitute for professional consultation. Readers experiencing mental health crisis, acute burnout, or concerns about their own or their child's wellbeing are advised to consult a qualified healthcare professional without delay.

The author and publisher make no representations or warranties of any kind regarding the accuracy, completeness, suitability, or applicability of the information contained herein. All content is provided in good faith based on available research at the time of writing. The author and publisher expressly disclaim liability for any loss, harm, or damage arising directly or indirectly from the use or application of any information, strategy, or tool presented in this book.

The case studies included in this publication are composites drawn from illustrative scenarios. All names used , including but not limited to Fenwick, Godric, Hadrian, Ivor, Jory, Kenrick, and Larkin , are entirely fictitious. Any resemblance to real individuals, living or deceased, is coincidental and unintentional. These narratives are constructed for illustrative purposes only and

Table of Contents

Preface

The burnout advice available to parents did not keep pace with the research.

For decades, recovery frameworks were built around a single premise: depletion is caused by doing too much, and restoration is caused by doing less. Rest more. Slow down. Practise self-care. The advice was well-intentioned, and for a certain population of parents in a certain type of household, it was adequate. For the growing population of late-diagnosed autistic and ADHD parents raising children with demand-based nervous systems, it consistently failed. Not because those parents were not trying. Because the advice was addressing the wrong system.

Autistic burnout is not the same as occupational burnout. The neuroscience literature has been clarifying this for the past decade, and the implications for recovery are substantial. The autistic nervous system depletes through sustained masking, sensory overload, and the absence of accommodation, and it restores through mechanisms that are specific to its profile and incompatible with the generic rest-and-self-care model. ADHD executive depletion compounds the picture: the systems most needed to identify burnout, plan a recovery response, and follow through on it are precisely the systems that ADHD burnout degrades first. Telling the ADHD parent to make better choices about their recovery is asking the depleted system to fix itself with the tools that depletion has specifically removed.

The PDA parenting layer adds a third dimension that the existing burnout literature does not address. Parenting a child with a Pathological Demand Avoidance profile requires a sustained, high-cost relational approach , low demand, collaborative, attuned , that draws specifically from the autistic and ADHD systems most depleted by the burnout it is helping to produce. The parent's burnout elevates the child's threat-detection system, which intensifies the parenting demand, which deepens the burnout. The mutual dysregulation cycle that results is not described in any mainstream parenting support framework, because mainstream parenting support frameworks were not built for this configuration.

This book is a response to that gap. It draws on autistic burnout research, ADHD executive function literature, PDA family studies, polyvagal theory, and self-compassion frameworks to construct a model specific to this parent and this household. The triple-layer burnout model, the non-negotiable audit, the three-tier recovery architecture, and the sustainable floor concept are all developed from the clinical evidence base and applied to the conditions that actually exist in these families. The case studies, all composite illustrations, are built from patterns documented across the lived experience literature rather than from any individual's account.

The book does not offer a resolution of the complexity of the AuDHD parenting experience. It offers a framework accurate enough to be useful within it. The distinction matters. Recovery that depends on the household being simpler than it is will fail at the first contact with reality. Recovery built around what the household actually contains has a chance of holding.

The research base for the specific combination of autistic burnout, ADHD depletion, and PDA parenting exhaustion is still developing. What exists is sufficient to build a working clinical picture, and that is what this book attempts to do , systematically, without shortcuts, in the language of the people it is written for.

The gap between the support that is available and the support that is needed in these families is substantial. The gap between what these parents have been told about themselves and what is factually true is equally substantial. Both of those gaps are worth naming precisely. That is what the following eleven chapters and six appendices attempt.

Introduction

What Burnout Actually Looks Like in This Household

You are probably not reading this in a calm moment. You are reading this because something in the last few weeks, or months, or possibly years, has stopped working. And it is not that you have not tried. That is the part nobody seems to understand. You have tried everything. You have read the books. You have attended the training. You have stayed up past midnight rereading the low-demand parenting guidance. You have tried softer language and fewer demands and more choices and longer repair conversations. And you are more exhausted now than when you started.

That exhaustion has a specific quality. It is not the tired you feel after a bad night's sleep. It is the kind of tired that sleep does not touch. You wake up already depleted. The morning feels like a task you do not have the resources to begin. Your capacity for problem-solving, which was never your most reliable asset, is now essentially absent. Things that used to be hard feel impossible. Things that used to be possible feel unbearable.

You may have been told you are burned out. You may have read that word in several places and thought: yes, that is it. But naming it has not changed anything. Because the advice that followed the word was the same advice it always is. Rest more. Ask for help. Set limits. Take care of yourself. And every time you read those instructions, something in you recognizes that they do not apply. Not to your household. Not to your nervous system. Not to your life.

This book starts from the assumption that you are right about that. The standard burnout advice was not built for you. This introduction is going to explain why, and then it is going to offer you a framework that actually accounts for what is happening in your body, in your brain, and in your household.

Why the Standard Burnout Advice Does Not Land

Burnout advice, as it is most commonly offered, rests on a few assumptions that go unstated because they seem obvious. It assumes that rest is accessible. That the person who is burned out can identify what they need. That once they have identified it, the system around them will accommodate it. That asking for help will produce useful help. That setting limits is a simple act of clear communication.

For the AuDHD parent of a PDA child, every one of those assumptions is wrong.

Rest requires executive function. You have to identify that you need it, make a plan to access it, communicate that plan to the people around you, and then actually stop doing the thing you were doing long enough for rest to occur. If your executive function is depleted, as ADHD depletion specifically produces, none of those steps are available. You cannot rest your way out of ADHD depletion in the same way you cannot lift yourself off the ground by pulling on your own collar.

Self-care requires interoception. It requires the ability to accurately read your own internal state, notice what it needs, and respond to it. For autistic people, interoception is frequently altered. Under autistic burnout, it becomes even less reliable. The body is sending signals. The burnout makes those signals harder to read, not easier. You are the last person in the room to notice how bad it has gotten, not because you are not paying attention, but because the system that would tell you has been running on fumes for months.

Setting limits with a demand-avoidant child is not a simple act. The PDA nervous system responds to limits as it responds to all demands: with resistance driven by anxiety, not defiance. You cannot set a firm limit with a PDA child the way the limit-setting advice assumes. You can reduce demands, offer choices, build in genuine autonomy. But the clean, confident limit-setting that restores order in neurotypical households is not available to you. And being told to set limits with your child while already in burnout is like being told to run a race while you are recovering from a broken leg.

Asking for help requires knowing what help would look like. It requires the cognitive capacity to analyze your situation, identify a specific form of support, communicate that need clearly, and receive the response without it creating more work than it solves. In burnout, that cognitive capacity is specifically what is missing. The people around you may be willing to help. But if they do not understand your household, their help will often miss the mark, sometimes badly enough to add to your load rather than reduce it.

This is the trap. The burnout removes the resources that would allow you to access the standard recovery tools. And the standard recovery tools were not designed for this nervous system or this household anyway.

The Triple-Layer Model: Three Depletion Systems at Once

What is happening in the AuDHD parent who is raising a PDA child is not a single burnout. It is three distinct depletion processes running simultaneously, each feeding the others.

The first layer is autistic burnout. Researchers at the Academic Autism Spectrum Partnership in Research and Education defined autistic burnout as a state of pervasive exhaustion, reduced ability to manage social and daily demands, and loss of skills, resulting from accumulated life stress and lack of adequate support (Raymaker et al., 2020). Autistic burnout is not depression, though it shares some features. It is not a standard stress response. It is a neurological consequence of long-term overload on a system that was never designed for the conditions it has been operating in. It shows up as heightened sensory sensitivity, loss of previously held skills, reduced cognitive processing, and a flattening of emotional range that can feel like numbness or like nothing working quite right.

The second layer is ADHD depletion. Researcher Russell Barkley has described executive function as the capacity to manage behavior across time toward future goals, and documented how that capacity degrades under conditions of sustained demand, poor sleep, high emotional load, and absent reward (Barkley, 2012). ADHD depletion is the collapse of the dopamine-dependent systems that govern initiation, planning, working memory, and emotional regulation. It shows up as an inability to start tasks you want to complete, time blindness that gets worse under stress, emotional responses that feel disproportionate, and a specific kind of paralysis where you know what you need to do and cannot make your body do it.

The third layer is PDA parenting exhaustion. This is the specific cost of maintaining a low-demand, autonomy-supportive household as a parent whose own nervous system requires structure, routine, and predictability to function. The low-demand approach to PDA parenting asks you to reduce your visible expectations of your child, offer genuine choice at every decision point, stay calm when things escalate, repair without blame, and sustain all of this across the full unpredictable range of your child's nervous system day. That is a profound and ongoing demand. For the AuDHD parent, it is not just effortful. It requires the precise resources that autistic burnout and ADHD depletion have already removed.

These three depletion systems do not operate in parallel. They share a nervous system. When autistic burnout lowers your sensory threshold, the noise of PDA parenting becomes more acute, which accelerates the burnout. When ADHD depletion removes your executive strategies, the cognitive load of maintaining low-demand parenting increases, which deepens the depletion. When PDA parenting exhaustion consumes the hours and energy that might otherwise have restored you, both the autistic burnout and the ADHD depletion accelerate.

Here is how that triple-layer depletion showed up for one parent.

Consider Aldwyn (name changed), a parent in his early forties who had been diagnosed with ADHD in his mid-thirties and had received an autism assessment in the previous year. His daughter, who was eleven at the time he came to this framework, had a PDA profile that had been recognized formally four years earlier. Aldwyn described himself as someone who had always managed, had always found a way through, had always developed systems that mostly worked. He had read the PDA parenting guides. He had implemented the strategies. He had made real changes to how he communicated and what he expected from his daughter. And then, in the space of about six months, the systems stopped working. He could not initiate. He could not recover from small upsets. He was more sensitive to noise and light than he had ever been. He was not depressed. He was not anxious in the way he understood anxiety. He was simply, and pervasively, out of resource. When he encountered the triple-layer model, what he described was not a moment of discovery so much as a moment of recognition. All three of the layers were already familiar. He had read about autistic burnout and recognized himself in it. He had read about ADHD executive function collapse and recognized himself in it. He had read about PDA parenting exhaustion and recognized himself in it. What he had never seen was all three described as a single interacting system. That description was what changed things. Not because it told him what to do, but because it told him what was actually happening. The previous advice had treated one layer at a time. The triple-layer model told him why addressing one layer at a time had never been enough.

What This Book Is and What It Is Not

This book is a practical recovery framework for the triple-layer burnout specific to AuDHD parents of PDA children. It addresses all three depletion systems simultaneously because that is the only approach that has any chance of working. It does not ask you to try harder. It does not assume that if you just applied the strategies more consistently you would be fine. It starts from the factual position that the conditions you have been operating in are genuinely demanding, that your nervous system has been responding accurately to those conditions, and that the standard recovery tools were built for a different profile in a different household.

Psychologist Kristin Neff's research on self-compassion has consistently shown that the pressure people place on themselves to perform better under difficult conditions does not improve outcomes. It increases the physiological stress response and reduces the cognitive resources available for problem-solving (Neff, 2011). This book is built on the opposite approach. It starts by recognizing the conditions accurately. Then it builds recovery infrastructure that works with your nervous system rather than against it.

What this book is not: it is not a promise that things will become easy. PDA parenting is not a problem you solve. It is an ongoing, shifting, genuinely complex relationship that changes as your child grows and as you do. What this book offers is a way to stop operating at the edge of collapse and start operating at a sustainable level. That level may be lower than you want it to be. It will also be more stable than what you have now.

This book also does not replace professional support. If you or your child are in crisis, please reach out to a qualified professional. The framework here is designed to complement clinical support, not substitute for it.

How to Read This Book When You Are Already Running on Empty

The chapters in this book are designed to be read in any order. If Chapter 9.0 on simultaneous parental and child crisis is where you are right now, start there. If Chapter 5.0 on the non-negotiable audit is the most urgent thing, go there first. The book is built to stand up to non-linear reading from an executive-function-depleted brain.

Each chapter opens with a clear statement of purpose and closes with a summary. If you have read a chapter before and forgotten it, that is fine. Reading it again is the system working as designed.

The case studies throughout are composite fictional constructs based on real patterns. Names are fictional. They are there to show you that the things described in these pages happen to real people in real households, and to model how the concepts in each chapter connect to actual experience.

You do not have to take notes. You do not have to do the reflective exercises in order. Some people find it useful to write. Some find it more useful to sit with a question while they are making tea or walking around the block. Both work. What matters is that the material connects to your situation in some way that is practically useful.

The depth researcher David Milton documented the structural quality of the mismatch between autistic communication styles and neurotypical environments, describing what he termed the double empathy problem: the failure of understanding between neurotypes is bidirectional, not a deficit residing in the autistic person alone (Milton, 2012). The same structural mismatch applies to the standard support literature around burnout. It was built by and for a neurotypical experience. This book is a corrective to that gap. Use it in whatever way fits the brain you have.

A Note on Recovery

Recovery from triple-layer burnout is not a return to a previous state. For many AuDHD parents of PDA children, the previous state was itself unsustainable. What recovery means in this context is building a sustainable floor: a functional level you can maintain consistently, without periodic collapse, across the genuine complexity of your household.

That floor is probably lower than you want it to be. Most people, when they first hear that framing, feel some resistance to it. They do not want a lower standard. They want to be the parent they were trying to be before the burnout. This is understandable. It is also not how recovery works for this profile.

The sustainable floor is not a concession to failure. It is a realistic account of what the AuDHD nervous system can maintain under current conditions, and what adjustments to those conditions would allow the floor to gradually rise. The book will return to this concept in Chapter 10.0 in detail. For now, it is enough to know that the recovery being offered here is not a sprint back to the previous level. It is the construction of a different kind of stability: one that does not collapse.

The Foundation

This introduction has established three things that will shape everything that follows.

The standard burnout advice does not apply to this household because it was not built for this nervous system, this child, or these conditions. Rest is not accessible when executive function is depleted. Self-care is not accessible when interoception is impaired. Limit-setting is not available in the way it is assumed to be when the child is demand-avoidant.

The triple-layer model names what is actually happening: autistic burnout, ADHD depletion, and PDA parenting exhaustion are three distinct but interacting depletion systems running on the same nervous system, each accelerating the others.

Recovery in this context is not a return to a previous state. It is the construction of a sustainable floor, built on recovery architecture that operates without requiring the depleted system to access it through willpower.

The chapters ahead are built on those three foundations. They do not ask you to try harder. They ask you to understand the conditions more accurately, build infrastructure that fits the conditions, and start from the honest position that the system was always going to fail under the load it was being asked to carry.

That is not a failure of parenting. It is the predictable outcome of genuinely inadequate conditions.

Now let us start building something better.

Chapter 1.0 The Triple Layer Explained

Three Different Depletion Systems One Nervous System

Most frameworks for understanding burnout assume there is one thing happening. Accumulated stress. A depleted battery. A well that has run dry. The metaphors vary but the model underneath them is the same: one resource, one depletion process, one recovery pathway.

For the AuDHD parent of a PDA child, that model is wrong. It is not that you are more burned out than other people. It is that you are experiencing three distinct depletion processes at the same time, each with its own mechanism, its own signature, and its own specific recovery requirements. They happen to share a nervous system. They happen to compete for the same limited resources. And the collapse of any one of them accelerates the collapse of the other two.

Understanding why generic burnout advice does not work for you starts here. The advice was designed to address one depletion process. You have three. And they are not simply additive. They interact. They amplify. They create a cascade that is qualitatively different from what any single-layer burnout framework was designed to address.

This chapter names all three layers, describes how each one works, and explains the specific way they connect to and intensify each other. It is the conceptual foundation for everything that follows in this book. You do not need to take notes. You need to understand the model well enough to recognize yourself in it. Most people who encounter this framework for the first time describe the experience as recognition rather than revelation. It names something that was already there but had no accurate language.

Autistic Burnout: What It Actually Is

Autistic burnout is not a metaphor. It is a specific neurological state with a defined set of features that distinguish it from general exhaustion, from depression, and from the burnout described in occupational health literature.

Researchers Raymaker, Teo, and colleagues defined autistic burnout as a syndrome of pervasive, long-term exhaustion, loss of function, and reduced tolerance to stimuli that results from the accumulation of life stress and the absence of adequate support (Raymaker et al., 2020). Three features distinguish it from other states. First, the exhaustion is pervasive: it does not lift after rest in the way normal tiredness does. Second, there is skill loss: capacities that were previously available, things the person had learned to do and relied on, become temporarily inaccessible. Third, the sensory threshold drops: the person becomes significantly more sensitive to stimulation that they could previously tolerate.

For the AuDHD parent, autistic burnout looks like this. The noise that used to be manageable background sound now feels like a physical intrusion. The grocery shopping that required effort before now feels genuinely impossible, not because of a lack of willpower but because the cognitive and sensory processing required has temporarily exceeded what the depleted system can provide. Tasks that were in the difficult category move into the unavailable category. The emotional regulation that was always a managed process rather than an automatic one now fails in situations where it would previously have held.

There is a feature of autistic burnout that is particularly relevant for the parent who is also parenting a demand-avoidant child. Autistic burnout tends to reduce the capacity for the kind of flexible, adaptive, in-the-moment response that PDA parenting requires. Low-demand parenting is cognitively demanding work. It requires reading a child's nervous system accurately, adjusting communication in real time, holding back the instinct to insist, and finding indirect routes to necessary outcomes. These are high-cost cognitive operations under any conditions. During autistic burnout, they are often simply not available.

What causes autistic burnout? The research points to the cumulative cost of operating in environments and conditions that were not designed for the neurotype. Not dramatic single events, though those can contribute, but the ongoing background cost of masking, of sensory management, of social performance, of effortful processing that neurotypical people do not experience as effortful at all (Raymaker et al., 2020). That cost accumulates over time. Autistic burnout is what happens when the accumulated cost exceeds the available recovery.

ADHD Depletion: The Dopamine Drain

ADHD depletion is a different process. Where autistic burnout is primarily a response to chronic overload and absent support, ADHD depletion is the progressive collapse of a dopamine-dependent executive function system that has been running without adequate fuel.

Neuroscientist Nora Volkow and colleagues have documented the specific role of dopamine dysregulation in ADHD, showing that the dopamine systems that govern motivation, reinforcement, initiation, and effort are fundamentally altered in people with ADHD (Volkow et al., 2011). The ADHD nervous system does not generate the same automatic motivational responses to tasks and demands that the neurotypical nervous system does. It relies heavily on interest, urgency, novelty, challenge, and sometimes crisis to generate the dopamine that neurotypical nervous systems produce more reliably. When those conditions are present, the ADHD system can perform extraordinarily well. When they are absent, or when sustained demand without adequate reward has depleted the system over time, the result is what clinicians and people with ADHD both describe as an inability to do things you want to do, need to do, and know you should do.

ADHD depletion under chronic stress looks like this. Task initiation fails across the board, including for things that used to carry enough interest or urgency to self-generate. Working memory, already a weak point, becomes less reliable, so that instructions disappear mid-execution, steps are missed, and things that need to happen at specific times are lost entirely. Emotional dysregulation increases. Shaw and colleagues have documented the relationship between ADHD and emotion regulation difficulties, noting that the same executive systems that govern task management also govern the regulation of emotional responses, and when those systems are depleted, emotional responses become larger, faster, and harder to recover from (Shaw et al., 2014).

For the parent, ADHD depletion shows up as a specific kind of paralysis that is easily mistaken for laziness or depression. You are not sad. You are not unmotivated in the usual sense. You are looking at a task that matters to you and experiencing a genuine neurological inability to begin it. You are watching yourself fail to do things and the gap between what you understand needs to happen and your capacity to make it happen keeps widening.

This is important to name precisely because ADHD depletion is often the layer the AuDHD parent has been explaining to themselves in the harshest terms. They know they have ADHD. They have lived with the gap between intention and execution their whole lives. During depletion, they tend to interpret the widening of that gap as a character failing rather than as a system running critically low on the specific neurochemical resources it needs to function.

PDA Parenting Exhaustion: The Third Layer

The third depletion layer is specific to this family configuration. It is the cost that PDA parenting extracts from an AuDHD nervous system when that nervous system is the primary delivery mechanism for a sustained low-demand household.

To understand why this is a distinct layer rather than simply an aspect of parenting stress, it helps to understand what PDA parenting actually asks of the parent. A low-demand, autonomy-supportive approach to PDA requires the parent to consistently reduce the perceived demand load in all interactions with the child. This means indirect communication rather than direct requests. It means offering genuine choice at every decision point rather than direction. It means staying regulated when the child is dysregulated, because co-regulation is how the PDA nervous system returns to safety, and the parent's nervous system is the regulation resource the child is borrowing. It means repair after conflict without blame, without lengthy explanation, without the rehearsed accountability conversation that other parenting frameworks recommend. It means holding all of this consistently while the child's nervous system is producing behavior that in any other context would read as defiant, aggressive, or deliberately provocative.

For a neurotypical parent with adequate support, this is hard. For an AuDHD parent whose own nervous system requires structure, predictability, and clear boundaries to function, whose sensory system is already taxed by the ambient noise and unpredictability of a dysregulated household, and whose executive function is already under strain, it is a level of demand that the available resources were never designed to sustain indefinitely.

The specific exhaustion produced by PDA parenting in an AuDHD parent has some features that distinguish it from general parenting fatigue. The first is the cost of suppressed directness. Most AuDHD adults have a direct communication style that functions as a cognitive default. They process information directly and express it directly. PDA parenting requires chronic suppression of that default, which is itself a high-cost executive function operation. The second is the unpredictability cost. PDA households operate on the child's nervous system rather than on a predictable schedule, and unpredictability is specifically dysregulating for the AuDHD nervous system that relies on routine and predictability to maintain function. The third is the repair demand. PDA parenting generates more conflict and requires more repair than most other parenting contexts, and each repair interaction requires emotional regulation, perspective-taking, and careful language management, all of which are high-cost operations for the AuDHD system.

How the Three Systems Amplify Each Other

The three depletion layers would be demanding enough in isolation. What makes the triple-layer burnout qualitatively different from any single-layer burnout is the way they interact.

Autistic burnout lowers the sensory and cognitive threshold. When that threshold drops, the sensory environment of the PDA household becomes more costly to process. The child's noise, movement, and unpredictability, which were already demanding, now exceed the reduced threshold regularly. Each threshold-crossing event contributes to the autistic burnout and also triggers the kind of acute stress response that consumes the dopamine resources the ADHD system was already running low on.

ADHD depletion removes the compensatory executive strategies. Most AuDHD adults have developed sophisticated, often effortful systems for managing the demands their neurotype creates. Reminders, routines, environmental design, scripts for difficult interactions, workarounds for the executive function deficits that would otherwise derail daily life. These strategies require executive function to access and maintain. When ADHD depletion reduces the available executive function, the compensatory strategies fail first. The person is then dealing with both the original ADHD challenges and the loss of the scaffolding that had been managing them. This directly increases the cost of PDA parenting, because PDA parenting depends on many of the same executive strategies: flexibility, planning, working memory, emotional regulation.

PDA parenting exhaustion removes the recovery windows. Recovery from both autistic burnout and ADHD depletion requires time outside of high demand. It requires periods of low stimulation, low expectation, and low social and cognitive load. In the PDA household, those periods are structurally rare. The child's profile generates demand that cannot be scheduled around. Evenings after school are often the highest-demand period of the day. Weekends do not offer the predictable respite that school-aged children in other families provide. The windows that would allow restoration of autistic and ADHD depletion are specifically the windows that PDA parenting occupies.

The Cascade Pattern

When the three depletion systems have been running simultaneously for long enough without adequate recovery, a cascade pattern emerges. The parent is not simply more tired than they were last month. Each week they are functionally less capable than the week before, across multiple domains simultaneously.

The sensory threshold that was dropping now produces shutdowns or meltdowns that previously would not have occurred. The executive function that was reducing now fails at tasks that a few months ago were difficult but manageable. The emotional regulation that was always a managed rather than automatic process now fails consistently in interactions that previously produced adequate responses. The coping strategies that required effort to access are no longer accessible even with effort.

Stephen Porges's polyvagal theory offers a useful framework for understanding the physiology of this cascade. Porges documents how the autonomic nervous system operates through a hierarchy of responses, moving from the socially engaged ventral vagal state through the mobilized sympathetic state to the immobilized dorsal vagal state under conditions of persistent threat and failed recovery (Porges, 2011). What the cascade pattern describes from a lived experience perspective maps closely onto the autonomic system progressively losing access to the more sophisticated regulatory states and defaulting to the more primitive ones. The person becomes harder to regulate, less able to maintain the social engagement necessary for co-regulation with their child, and increasingly operating from a threat-detection state that has no reliable off switch.

The cascade is what most people who come to this book are actually in. They may not have recognized it as a cascade. They may have attributed it to poor character, depression, laziness, or simply the difficulty of the parenting situation. What they have experienced is a predictable neurological pattern in a system that has been running beyond its sustainable capacity for too long, without adequate recovery infrastructure.

Why You Cannot Recover From One While the Others Continue

This is the reason single-layer burnout interventions fail for the AuDHD parent of a PDA child.

Address the autistic burnout without addressing the ADHD depletion, and you may reduce the sensory overload temporarily, but the executive function system is still failing, which means the strategies needed to maintain the autistic burnout recovery will themselves fail. You cannot maintain a reduced-demand environment for your autistic nervous system if your ADHD executive function is too depleted to implement it.

Address the ADHD depletion without addressing PDA parenting exhaustion, and you may restore some executive function temporarily, but the recovery windows that would allow that restoration to consolidate are still being occupied by the ongoing demands of the household. The ADHD system cannot rebuild its dopamine resources faster than the PDA parenting is draining them.

Address the PDA parenting exhaustion without addressing autistic burnout, and you may reduce the visible parenting demand, but the autistic nervous system is still operating with a compromised threshold and a compromised capacity for flexible response. The reduced demand load does not restore the autistic system if the system has been operating below recovery threshold for long enough.

Recovery requires all three layers to receive simultaneous attention. Not equal attention at every moment, different layers may need priority at different points, but all three must be included in the recovery architecture. The chapters ahead address them as a system rather than as separate problems.

What the Model Means for Your Recovery

Understanding the triple-layer model changes what recovery looks like and what it does not look like.

It means recovery cannot be primarily additive. You cannot add rest to a depleted system and expect the added rest to outrun the ongoing depletion. You cannot add self-care to a system that does not have the resources to access it. Before recovery can begin, the demand load has to reduce. The chapters on triage, the non-negotiable audit, and the minimum viable household in this book address that reduction directly.

It means recovery requires a structure that does not depend on the depleted system to access it in real time. The classic burnout advice assumes the person can identify what they need and choose to do it. For the AuDHD parent in triple-layer depletion, that assumption fails at the exact moment when recovery is most needed. Recovery architecture, as this book describes it, has to be designed in advance and operate through environmental design rather than through real-time decision-making.

It means recovery is not measured against a pre-burnout standard. For many AuDHD parents, the pre-burnout state was itself operating close to the edge of sustainable function. Recovery does not mean returning to that state. It means building a sustainable floor, a functional level that can be maintained without periodic collapse, and that can gradually improve as the structural conditions improve.

Here is how the triple-layer model landed for one parent.

Consider Bramwell (name changed), who came to the triple-layer framework after two years of what he described as progressive functional collapse. He had a late autism diagnosis at thirty-eight and had been working with an ADHD diagnosis since his early twenties. His son had a PDA profile. Bramwell described the previous two years as baffling in retrospect because he had been doing more, not less, in terms of interventions. He had tried a sensory diet approach for his autistic burnout. He had tried stimulant medication adjustments for his ADHD. He had attended a PDA parenting course. Each of these helped, briefly, and then stopped helping. When Bramwell mapped his two years against the triple-layer model, what emerged was a clear picture of a cascade he had been treating one layer at a time. The sensory diet reduced his autistic overload but was implemented through a structured daily routine that his ADHD executive function could not sustain once the novelty faded. The medication adjustment restored some initiation capacity but the recovery windows that would have allowed him to use that capacity were occupied by escalated parenting demands during the same period. The PDA parenting course gave him better strategies but those strategies required the kind of flexible, regulated, low-threshold response that his autistic burnout had specifically removed. Looking at it as a single interacting system was the first time the pattern made sense to him. He had not been failing to recover. He had been recovering in one layer while the other two continued to deplete. The model did not tell him what to do. But it told him why nothing had worked, and that changed the nature of the question he was trying to answer.

The Foundation of the Chapters Ahead

Three depletion systems share a nervous system in the AuDHD
parent of a PDA child. Autistic burnout is the neurological
consequence of chronic overload and absent support,
characterised by pervasive exhaustion, skill loss, and a dropped
sensory threshold. ADHD depletion is the progressive collapse of
the dopamine-dependent executive function system under
sustained demand without adequate recovery, characterised by
failed initiation, widened emotional dysregulation, and the loss of
the compensatory strategies that had been managing the ADHD
challenges. PDA parenting exhaustion is the specific cost of
maintaining a low-demand household as a parent whose own
nervous system requires structure, predictability, and clear
communication to function.

The three systems amplify each other. The cascade pattern that
results when all three have been running below recovery
threshold is not a character failing or a parenting inadequacy. It is
the predictable neurological outcome of a system operating
beyond its sustainable capacity without the specific recovery
infrastructure it requires.

Recovery addresses all three layers simultaneously. That is what
this book is for.

Chapter 2.0 Recognising Your Own Burnout

Why Recognition Is Harder Than It Sounds

If you could see your own burnout clearly, you would not need a chapter on recognising it. The reason recognition is difficult is not carelessness or inattention. It is structural. The AuDHD nervous system under burnout is specifically impaired in the domains that recognition requires: accurate reading of internal states, realistic self-assessment, and the kind of cognitive stepping-back that allows pattern recognition over time.

There is a particular irony in the recognition problem. The person who most needs to recognise that they are in triple-layer burnout is the same person whose burnout has specifically degraded the tools they would use to recognise it. The interoception that would report the physiological state is impaired by autistic burnout. The executive function that would allow pattern recognition across time is depleted by ADHD depletion. The cognitive clarity that would allow accurate self-assessment is reduced by both. And underneath all of that, there is the masking.

This chapter is about giving you external markers to use when the internal ones are not available. It distinguishes the signals of autistic burnout from the signals of ADHD depletion from the signals of PDA parenting exhaustion, because the signals look different and they point to different recovery priorities. It closes with a self-assessment framework you can return to monthly as a monitoring tool, not just as a one-time check.

The Masking Trap: Still Functioning While Depleted

Most autistic adults who were not diagnosed in childhood developed masking as a survival strategy. Masking is the learned suppression of neurological difference in social and professional contexts: performing neurotypical communication styles, managing visible stimming or sensory responses, producing the expected emotional and social cues regardless of the actual internal state. It is cognitively expensive. It is socially effective, at least in the short term. And it continues to run during burnout.

Cage and Troxell-Whitman's research on masking found that higher levels of camouflaging neurological difference were associated with significantly higher rates of anxiety, depression, and reduced quality of life, and that the relationship held even after controlling for autistic trait severity (Cage and Troxell-Whitman, 2019). The mechanism is direct: masking is a resource drain that does not produce the social return it promises. The person pays the cost and the neurotype remains, requiring ongoing suppression.

For the AuDHD parent in burnout, masking creates a recognition trap. The external performance of functioning continues past the point where the internal resources have been exhausted. They are still showing up for work. They are still responding to messages. They are still producing the social cues that register as managing. The people around them, including sometimes their partner and sometimes their therapist, read the external performance and do not see the depletion underneath it.

The AuDHD parent is usually the last person to update the internal assessment. They use the same external performance as evidence. Still functioning, they tell themselves. Not that bad yet. Other people manage worse. The bar for acknowledging that they are not managing keeps receding.

The masking trap means that burnout recognition for this profile almost always comes later than it should, and at a more acute point than it would for someone whose external state more accurately reflects their internal one. This chapter is partly about helping you see past the performance to the signals it is hiding.

Autistic Burnout Signals in the AuDHD Parent

The autistic burnout signals are the ones most likely to be attributed to other causes. They overlap with sensory processing differences that were always present, which makes them easy to dismiss as baseline rather than as change. But they are changes, and watching for the direction of change is what matters.

The sensory threshold signal. Things that were previously tolerable are no longer tolerable. The television volume that was background noise now needs to be off. The texture of certain clothing is newly unbearable. Fluorescent lighting that could be managed with effort is now producing headaches or shutdowns. This is not increased sensitivity as a fixed trait. It is the threshold dropping as the autistic system moves deeper into burnout.

The skill regression signal. Tasks that were previously in the difficult-but-available category have moved into unavailable. This often shows up in communication: written communication becomes harder to produce, verbal communication in unfamiliar situations requires more recovery time, the social scripts that were automated enough to run on low fuel now fail mid-execution. It may also show up in practical capacities: driving routes that were reliable become confusing, familiar administrative tasks require more steps to complete than they used to.

The recovery time signal. The time required to recover from stimulating or demanding events has increased. A social event that previously required a quiet afternoon to recover from now requires several days. A child meltdown that previously required a short decompression now produces an exhaustion that lasts until the following day. The recovery arc is longer and the person comes back from it at a lower baseline than before.

The emotional narrowing signal. The emotional range available has compressed. Things that would previously have produced pleasure, connection, or genuine engagement now produce neutrality or a kind of flat affect. This is not depression in the clinical sense, though it may resemble it. It is the autistic system protecting its remaining resources by reducing the processing allocated to non-essential emotional responses.

ADHD Depletion Signals: From the Inside

The ADHD depletion signals are the ones most likely to be interpreted through the lens of shame. Because the ADHD parent already knows they have executive function difficulties, they tend to absorb the depletion signals into their existing self-concept as someone who struggles, and miss the fact that the degree of struggle has changed significantly.

The initiation failure signal. This is the most recognizable ADHD depletion signal and the hardest to distinguish from the baseline ADHD experience. The distinction is in degree and spread. Standard ADHD initiation difficulty is selective: it affects certain tasks, in certain conditions, and the person has developed workarounds for the most affected areas. Depletion-level initiation failure spreads across categories that were previously available. The person cannot start the task they genuinely want to do. They cannot initiate the phone call they have been looking forward to making. Initiation failure is no longer selective. It is pervasive.

The working memory acceleration signal. Working memory in ADHD is always compromised. Under depletion, it becomes significantly more unreliable. Instructions disappear between reception and execution. The plan that was clear ten minutes ago is now inaccessible. Multiple-step tasks fail consistently at the transition between steps. The person finds themselves standing in a room with no memory of why they went there, multiple times a day rather than occasionally.

The emotional velocity signal. Barkley's research on executive function has documented the role of executive systems in the regulation of emotional responses, noting that the inhibitory systems that in neurotypical people produce a gap between stimulus and response are less reliable in ADHD (Barkley, 1997).

Under depletion, that gap narrows further. Emotional responses arrive faster, are larger in relation to the stimulus, and the recovery from them is slower. The AuDHD parent finds themselves having a response to a minor frustration that feels disproportionate and that they have no available resource to modulate in the moment.

The interest system collapse signal. Under depletion, the ADHD interest system, which is the primary driver of sustained engagement and the main source of dopamine reward, becomes less responsive. Things that were reliably interesting no longer generate engagement. The special interest that usually provides restoration does not activate in the same way. The parent notices they are not enjoying things they always enjoyed, and unlike the autistic burnout version of this signal, the ADHD version carries a specific quality of flatness rather than narrowing.

PDA Parenting Exhaustion: The Specific Markers

The PDA parenting exhaustion signals are the ones most likely to go entirely unnamed, because there is almost no existing literature that describes them as a distinct category.

The indirectness cost signal. The AuDHD parent who has been maintaining indirect communication with their PDA child begins to notice the cost accumulating as a specific kind of communication fatigue. The direct statement that would take two seconds of cognitive effort requires ten seconds of reframing, checking, adjusting, and delivery monitoring. Over the course of a day's interactions, that difference in cost becomes significant. The parent notices they are beginning to avoid communication with their child, not from lack of love or care, but from the sheer depletion of the indirectness cost.

The regulation lending signal. Co-regulation with a dysregulated PDA child requires the parent to maintain a regulated state while in proximity to a nervous system that is actively broadcasting dysregulation. This is the autonomic equivalent of generating body heat to warm a cold room: the room may warm slightly but the person producing the heat gets colder. The parent notices they are increasingly dysregulated after co-regulation attempts rather than returning to baseline, and that the dysregulation from one interaction carries into the next.

The anticipatory monitoring signal. PDA parenting requires constant ambient awareness of the child's current nervous system state, demand load, and likely trajectory. This is not the same as simply being attentive to your child. It is a sustained, resource-intensive monitoring operation that runs in the background of everything else the parent does. Under exhaustion, that monitoring becomes intrusive: the parent cannot set it down even during periods when the child is settled. They are monitoring for threat in the PDA household even when no active threat is present, which is itself a significant resource drain.

The repair depletion signal. PDA parenting generates more conflict and therefore more repair demand than most other parenting configurations. Each repair interaction, done well, requires regulated presence, accurate empathy, carefully chosen language, and patience with the pace at which the PDA nervous system moves through repair. Under exhaustion, the parent begins to notice they are avoiding repair, or attempting it too quickly, or losing regulation during it, not because they do not want to repair, but because the repair resources have been depleted.

The Signs You Are Most Likely to Miss

Three signals cross the layers and are consistently the most underidentified. The first is increased rigidity. AuDHD adults are often flexible thinkers within their areas of interest and competence, and may have a self-concept as adaptable rather than rigid. But under triple-layer burnout, the need for predictability and control in the environment increases significantly, as the system attempts to reduce the cognitive load of processing novelty and unpredictability. The parent may not recognise the increasing rigidity as a burnout signal because it runs against their self-concept.

The second is social withdrawal that looks like preference. The AuDHD parent in burnout often withdraws from social contact, but frames it as a preference for time alone rather than as a signal that social interaction has become too costly to sustain. The withdrawal is real and may even be partially restorative, but if it is progressive and if it is accompanied by a loss of the enjoyment of interactions that were previously genuinely wanted, it is a burnout signal, not a preference.

The third is the loss of time sense about the burnout itself. Parham and Ecker have documented the relationship between sensory processing differences and altered time perception under stress conditions (Parham and Ecker, 2007). Under burnout, the AuDHD parent often loses accurate tracking of how long they have been depleted. They may say they have been struggling for a few weeks when the burnout markers, if traced backwards, show a pattern of many months. This matters for recovery, because the length and depth of the burnout affects what recovery architecture is required.

Your Current Burnout Profile: A Self-Assessment

The self-assessment in Appendix A provides the full version of this tool. The framework here is a rapid orientation to which of the three layers is currently most acute, to help you identify where in this book to direct your attention first.

For each of the three clusters below, notice how many of the markers are currently present and how intense they are.

The autistic burnout cluster: sensory threshold has dropped in the past three months; skills or capacities that were previously available have become unreliable or unavailable; recovery time after demanding events has increased significantly; emotional range has narrowed or flattened; the period between adequate sensory environment and overload has shortened.

The ADHD depletion cluster: initiation failure has spread to categories that were previously available; working memory is failing more frequently and more significantly than baseline; emotional responses are arriving faster and recovering more slowly; the interest system is less responsive and the things that usually restore engagement are not working.

The PDA parenting exhaustion cluster: communication with your child is increasingly costly; you are less regulated after co-regulation attempts than before them; you are monitoring your child's nervous system state even during settled periods; repair is being avoided or rushed; you are managing your child's experience of demand with significantly more effort than six months ago.

Whichever cluster contains the most markers, or the most intense markers, is your current priority layer. That does not mean the others are not present. It means the chapter and tools in this book most directly relevant to your current state are organised around that layer.

What Your Body Has Already Been Telling You

The body's burnout signals are often the most reliable data available, and the most consistently ignored.

Raymaker and colleagues noted that participants describing autistic burnout frequently reported physical symptoms as part of the burnout experience, including increased illness, pain, fatigue, and physical shutdown (Raymaker et al., 2020). This aligns with what the polyvagal framework predicts: when the autonomic nervous system is running in a sustained threat-detection state, the physiological systems that require a settled state to function well, including the immune system, the digestive system, and the musculoskeletal system, operate less effectively.

For the AuDHD parent, the body's burnout signals are worth attending to specifically because the interoceptive alterations common in autism mean the cognitive recognition of burnout often lags well behind the physiological reality. The jaw that has been clenched for weeks. The gut that has been unreliable. The shoulders that will not release. The recurring headaches or the recurrent minor illnesses. These are not incidental. They are the body reporting a state that the cognitive system may not yet have accurately registered.

The self-assessment in Appendix A includes a physical signals section for this reason. Tracking the physical signals alongside the cognitive and behavioral ones gives a more complete picture of where the three depletion systems currently are than any single category of observation can produce.

Here is how this recognition process worked for one parent.

Consider Crispin (name changed), a woman in her mid-thirties with AuDHD who had been parenting her PDA-profile son for six years. She came to this book specifically because of PDA parenting exhaustion. She had read widely about PDA, had been implementing low-demand approaches for three years, and felt that she had reached the end of her capacity to sustain them. She expected the self-assessment to confirm that the PDA parenting exhaustion layer was her primary depletion. It did not. When she worked through the three clusters, the ADHD depletion cluster lit up with a density of markers she had not anticipated. The initiation failure that she had attributed to laziness for years. The working memory failures she had been managing with elaborate external systems that had recently started breaking down. The emotional velocity that had been increasing for months and that she had been treating as a response to the parenting situation rather than as a depletion signal in its own right. The PDA parenting exhaustion was real and was present. But the ADHD depletion was the more acute current state, and it had been depleting the resources she needed to sustain the PDA parenting work. Understanding that sequence changed her recovery priorities. She did not stop addressing the PDA parenting context. But she started by building the ADHD depletion recovery infrastructure first, because that layer was undermining everything else.

What This Chapter Has Named

Recognition is the prerequisite for recovery. You cannot address a depletion system you have not accurately identified.

The masking trap delays recognition because the external performance of functioning continues past the point where the internal resources are gone. Breaking through the masking trap requires looking at specific physiological and functional signals rather than at the overall performance level.

The three layers produce distinct signal clusters. Autistic burnout signals cluster around sensory threshold, skill regression, recovery time, and emotional narrowing. ADHD depletion signals cluster around initiation failure, working memory decline, emotional velocity, and interest system collapse. PDA parenting exhaustion signals cluster around indirectness cost, regulation lending, anticipatory monitoring, and repair depletion.

The self-assessment identifies your current priority layer. That does not mean the others are absent. It identifies where to direct your recovery attention first.

Your body has been tracking the burnout longer than your cognitive awareness has. The physical signals are data. The chapter ahead begins building the framework for what to do with it.

Chapter 3.0 Why You Cannot Just Rest

The Rest Instruction and Why It Fails Here

Of all the advice given to burned-out people, rest is the most universal and the most poorly fitted to this particular situation. It appears in almost every burnout resource. It is recommended by doctors, therapists, partners, and well-meaning friends. It sounds like the obvious answer. Stop doing so much. Give the system time to recover. Rest.

For the AuDHD parent of a PDA child, the rest instruction fails not because rest is wrong in theory but because the conditions it assumes are not present. The advice assumes that the person can access a genuine resting state. It assumes that lying down or taking time off will move the nervous system from activation to recovery. It assumes that the environment will allow quiet, that the brain will allow stillness, and that the system will respond to reduced input by beginning to restore. None of those assumptions hold reliably for this profile, and some of them fail specifically because of the burnout itself.

This chapter does not argue against rest. It argues against the generic rest instruction, which pretends that rest is a single, accessible, universally effective thing. For the AuDHD parent in triple-layer burnout, rest is a category that contains very different experiences with very different effects. Some of those experiences restore. Many of them do not. Understanding the difference is not a luxury. It is the difference between spending three days resting and feeling worse at the end of them and spending thirty minutes on the right activity and feeling the first genuine shift in weeks.

What Rest Requires That Burnout Takes Away

Genuine rest, in the physiological sense, requires a specific set of internal conditions. The autonomic nervous system needs to move out of the sympathetic threat-response state and into the parasympathetic rest-and-restore state. The body needs to register safety at a neurological level, not just a cognitive one. The mind needs to release the active monitoring of threat.

None of those transitions are automatic for the AuDHD parent, and all of them are specifically impaired by the triple-layer burnout.

The autistic nervous system that is in burnout is running with a lowered sensory threshold. In that state, the ambient environment is more threatening rather than less: sounds are louder, light is brighter, textures are more intrusive, the background noise of the household registers as acute input rather than neutral backdrop. Lying down in a burnout state does not remove those inputs. It often makes them more prominent because the task engagement that was providing some distraction is now absent. The person lies down and the sensory environment crowds in. The body is horizontal but the nervous system is not resting.

The ADHD system that is depleted carries a specific relationship with stillness. In motion, in task, in engagement, the ADHD nervous system has something to metabolize the excess activation. At rest, the activation remains but the task is gone. The thoughts that were manageable during activity become louder. The undone things that were compartmentalized during busyness surface one after another. The awareness of all the things that should be happening and are not happening fills the space that the task vacated. This is not anxiety in the clinical diagnostic sense, though it can feel identical. It is the ADHD nervous system in an environment with insufficient stimulation to regulate itself.

The PDA parenting household does not have reliable rest windows. The demand-avoidant child's nervous system does not accommodate the parent's scheduled recovery time. The parent who has announced a rest period has introduced a demand into the household: the demand for the child to manage without them, to be quieter than usual, to respect a boundary that the PDA nervous system will read as a constraint on autonomy. The rest period that was supposed to reduce demand has often increased it.

The Executive Function Cost of Accessing Rest

There is a precondition to rest that the rest instruction never mentions: you have to be able to access it. Accessing rest is not nothing. It requires executive function.

To rest genuinely, the AuDHD parent has to identify that they need rest, distinguish this kind of tired from the other kinds of tired, decide to pursue rest over the competing demands that are more visible and feel more urgent, communicate this decision to the people around them in a way that is likely to produce the conditions they need, transition away from active engagement toward a lower-demand state, and tolerate the discomfort of that transition without the executive function looping back to the undone tasks.

Every one of those steps requires the executive function that ADHD depletion has specifically reduced. The parent who most needs rest is the parent who is least able to work through the decision-making chain that leads to it.

Barkley has documented how ADHD executive function difficulties include not just task management but the management of transitions, the regulation of internal states, and the capacity for self-directed behavior in the absence of external structure or immediate reward (Barkley, 2012). Rest is self-directed behavior with no external structure and no immediate reward. It is the thing most likely to fall through the gap that ADHD depletion opens. The parent intends to rest and ends up doing something else, not because they are irresponsible but because the executive pathway between the intention and the action has a gap in it that the depletion widened.

Sensory Rest vs Cognitive Rest vs Emotional Rest

Part of what makes the generic rest instruction so consistently unhelpful is that it treats rest as a single thing. The AuDHD parent who is depleted across three layers is depleted in at least three different ways, each of which requires a different type of input withdrawal to begin restoring.

Sensory rest is the withdrawal of sensory input to below the threshold at which the sensory system is generating cost. For an autistic parent in burnout, this means something specific: not just quiet, but the right kind of quiet. Not just low light, but the right kind of low light. Not just less happening, but fewer of the specific sensory inputs that have been most costly. Sensory rest is not generic calm. It is calibrated reduction based on the particular sensory processing profile of the specific person. What counts as sensory rest for one autistic parent may be the sensory equivalent of noise for another.

Cognitive rest is the withdrawal from sustained, effortful cognitive processing. The mental load of PDA parenting, the anticipatory monitoring, the real-time communication adjustment, the repair planning, the school email writing, the medication management, the sensory management of the household environment: these are all cognitive activities that continue running even when the parent is nominally off duty. Cognitive rest requires that monitoring to actually stop. Not to be interrupted but to genuinely stop. For the parent whose cognitive system has been maintaining the household, the threshold between cognitive activity and cognitive rest is not a simple off switch.

Emotional rest is the withdrawal from the sustained emotional processing that the PDA parenting relationship requires. The parent who co-regulates a dysregulated child multiple times a day is doing sustained emotional labour at a level that most support frameworks do not recognise. Emotional rest is not the absence of feeling. It is the absence of the requirement to produce, manage, and sustain specific emotional states for the benefit of someone else's nervous system.

These three types of rest can be simultaneous but they do not have to be. And confusing them produces the experience many AuDHD parents report: of resting in one domain while continuing to deplete in another. The parent who takes a sensory rest by lying in a dark room but who is mentally processing the morning's difficult interaction is resting sensorially and depleting cognitively and emotionally at the same time.

When Rest Increases Anxiety Instead of Reducing It

A pattern that many AuDHD parents report but rarely see named is that rest, as they have been able to access it, increases their anxiety rather than reducing it. They lie down and feel worse. They take a day off and feel more overwhelmed by Monday than they did by Friday. They give themselves a break and find the break harder to tolerate than the activity it replaced.

This is not a psychological quirk. It has a neurological explanation at each of the three depletion layers.

Stephen Porges's polyvagal theory describes the conditions under which the autonomic nervous system can move into genuinely restorative states (Porges, 2011). The ventral vagal engaged state, the state in which genuine rest and restoration are physiologically possible, is not entered through the removal of stimulation. It is entered through the presence of safety cues. The system needs to register that there is no threat, not just that there is less input. For the parent whose nervous system has been in a sustained threat-detection state, the removal of activity does not automatically produce the safety signal. It removes the structure that was giving the activation somewhere to go, while leaving the activation itself in place. The result is a free-floating state of alert without object, which is experienced as anxiety, restlessness, or dread.

Kessler and colleagues documented the relationship between ADHD and chronic sleep disruption, finding that the cognitive and physiological activation that characterises ADHD does not reliably downregulate at rest or at the transition to sleep in the way it does for neurotypical people (Kessler et al., 2006). The ADHD brain at rest is not necessarily quieter than the ADHD brain at work. It is often louder. The tasks that were manageable during the day crowd into the rest period. The activation that the tasks were metabolizing becomes uncontained.

Daniel Siegel's work on interpersonal neurobiology describes how the relational nervous system of a primary caregiver becomes entrained to the arousal level of the child they are regulating (Siegel, 2012). For the parent who has been co-regulating a dysregulated PDA child throughout the day, their own nervous system has been locked at a relatively high activation level for extended periods. When the child goes to bed or has an unexpected quiet period, the parent's nervous system does not immediately drop to a lower state. It maintains the high-activation set point, looking for the next dysregulation event, monitoring for the signals that it has learned will come. Rest in that state is like trying to sleep on a moving train. The body is still.

ADHD and the Rest Paradox

There is a specific paradox in the ADHD relationship with rest that is worth naming separately because it produces a pattern that many parents recognise but cannot explain.

The ADHD nervous system needs more stimulation than the neurotypical nervous system to achieve the same level of regulation. It is chronically underaroused rather than overaroused, which is why stimulant medication increases calm rather than increasing activation. This means that the standard rest recommendation, reduce stimulation, reduce activity, give the system less to process, moves the ADHD nervous system in the direction of dysregulation rather than regulation. The parent who follows the rest instruction experiences an increase in restlessness, in the urge to do something, in the sense that lying still is physically intolerable.

This is not a discipline problem. It is the nervous system doing exactly what ADHD nervous systems do when stimulation is below their regulatory threshold. The rest instruction was designed for a nervous system that is overaroused and needs less. The ADHD nervous system needs different, not less.

The rest-adjacent activities that actually restore the ADHD nervous system often look, from the outside, like anything other than rest: a special interest, a repetitive physical activity, a low-stakes creative project, a familiar piece of media watched for the fourth time. These activities provide the right kind of stimulation to bring the nervous system to its regulatory level while reducing the emotional and cognitive demand load. They are not the absence of activity. They are activity that feeds rather than drains.

The PDA Household Problem

Even if all the other conditions for rest were in place, the PDA household creates a structural problem for parental recovery that is rarely acknowledged in burnout frameworks.

Standard recovery advice assumes that the person can create and protect recovery windows. They can communicate a need for rest to the people around them and those people will respond by reducing their demands. In a PDA household, this chain breaks at multiple points.

The communication of a rest need is itself a demand on the PDA child: the demand to manage differently during that period. The

PDA nervous system responds to implicit and explicit demands with anxiety-driven avoidance. The parent who says, I need some time to rest, I need you to play quietly for an hour, has introduced exactly the kind of demand the child's nervous system is most likely to respond to with increased behavior rather than decreased.

The unpredictability of the PDA household means that rest windows cannot be reliably scheduled. The parent who blocked Tuesday afternoon for recovery cannot predict whether Tuesday afternoon will be manageable or whether it will be the highest-demand period of the week. Planning rest in a PDA household requires accepting that the plan will frequently not be executed.

The PDA parent's own demand sensitivity, which is an aspect of their AuDHD profile, interacts with the difficulty of accessing rest in ways that are rarely addressed. The demand to rest, the cultural pressure that you should be doing self-care, you should be making time for yourself, can itself activate demand avoidance in the AuDHD parent. The very category of self-care as an obligation can become a source of demand resistance rather than a resource.

What Actually Restores the Three Systems

The replacement for the generic rest instruction is a set of specific inputs, one for each depletion layer, that move that layer toward restoration rather than further depletion.

For autistic burnout, restoration requires reduced cost input rather than zero input. The autistic system does not need silence and stillness. It often does not tolerate silence and stillness. It needs stimulation that is below the cost threshold: familiar, predictable, controllable, and not requiring active social or emotional processing. Special interests serve this function. Familiar media serves this function. Repetitive sensory input that is pleasurable rather than intrusive serves this function. The key variable is not the quantity of stimulation but the cost per unit.

For ADHD depletion, restoration requires input that matches the dopamine needs of the depleted system without adding to the executive demand load. This often means activities that carry their own inherent interest or reward, that do not require initiation effort across multiple steps, and that do not produce the guilt or anxiety of active avoidance. The thirty-minute special interest session is a better dopamine restoration tool than the two-hour nap because it actively replenishes the dopamine deficit rather than simply waiting for it to resolve.

For PDA parenting exhaustion, restoration requires the absence of the relational demand structure. This is distinct from social withdrawal. It is specifically the removal of the need to monitor, adjust, co-regulate, or repair in relation to another person's nervous system. Time that is not organised around someone else's state. This may look like solitude or it may look like low-stakes social connection with people who do not require the parent to manage their experience. The distinguishing factor is the absence of the monitoring obligation.

Rest-Adjacent Activities That Work

The most reliable restoration activities for AuDHD parents in triple-layer burnout share a set of features regardless of what the activity looks like on the surface. They are intrinsically motivating rather than externally obligated. They engage the nervous system at the right level: enough stimulation to prevent the ADHD anxiety of understimulation, not so much that the autistic threshold is breached. They remove the relational demand structure. They are repeatable without requiring re-initiation energy. And they do not generate guilt or the awareness of competing obligations while in progress.

Common examples that meet these criteria for different parents include: solitary special interest engagement, particularly when the interest is sedentary or low-motor; familiar television or film rewatching at low volume; repetitive physical activities such as walking, swimming, or rocking that provide proprioceptive input without cognitive demand; creative activities that do not have a performance standard, that is, making something with no audience; listening to familiar music or podcasts while doing low-demand tasks like tidying.

These are not the same as rest in the conventional sense. They will not be recognized as rest by a therapist who recommends rest as treatment. But they meet the actual physiological criteria for restoration more reliably than an afternoon lying down in a room that feels either too loud or too quiet, doing nothing while the activation level of the nervous system stays where it was.

Here is how this worked for one parent.

Consider Dunstan (name changed), a parent in his late thirties with late-diagnosed autism and a longstanding ADHD diagnosis, whose ten-year-old daughter had a PDA profile. Dunstan had been told by multiple professionals to rest more. He had tried. He had taken days off and found them more exhausting than the days he worked. He had attempted weekend lie-ins and found himself more functionally impaired on Monday than he had been on Friday. He had tried mindfulness and had spent the sessions in escalating internal noise rather than stillness. He had concluded that rest did not work for him, which he attributed to a character failing. When he began tracking his actual state across different activities, he found something he had not expected. The activity after which he most reliably felt better was a thirty-minute solo session with his model railway. He had not counted this as rest because it was not horizontal, it was not passive, and it was not what any professional had ever suggested. When he mapped it against the restoration framework, it met every criterion. Intrinsically motivating. Below the sensory cost threshold. Repetitive and familiar enough to require no executive initiation effort. Completely absent of relational demand. Dopamine-generating through the combination of interest and completion. He began protecting that thirty-minute window as a deliberate recovery tool rather than an occasional indulgence. The cumulative effect over six weeks was more measurable than anything a conventional rest approach had produced. The recovery it provided was not dramatic. But it was real. And it was repeatable. And it worked specifically because it was calibrated to what his three depletion systems actually needed rather than what the generic rest instruction assumed they needed.

What This Chapter Has Named

The generic rest instruction fails the AuDHD parent of a PDA child because it assumes conditions that are not present and a neurological response that does not reliably occur for this profile.

Rest in the conventional sense requires the nervous system to register safety. For the autistic system in burnout, the sensory environment may not allow that transition. For the ADHD system in depletion, removing stimulation increases dysregulation rather than reducing it. For the PDA household, rest windows cannot be reliably created or protected.

The three depletion systems each require specific inputs for restoration, not the absence of all inputs. Autistic burnout restores through low-cost, familiar, controllable stimulation. ADHD depletion restores through intrinsically rewarding activity that meets the dopamine needs of the depleted system. PDA parenting exhaustion restores through the removal of the relational monitoring and adjustment demand specifically.

Rest-adjacent activities that meet those criteria are not lesser alternatives to real rest. They are more effective restorative tools for this specific profile than the horizontal stillness that the word rest usually implies.

The next chapter moves from how the burnout affects the internal experience to how it shows up in the physical body, and why the body's burnout signals are often more reliable than the cognitive ones.

Chapter 4.0 The Body Keeps the Burnout

What Burnout Does to the Physical Body

When burnout is discussed in clinical settings, it is most often framed in terms of cognitive and emotional symptoms: exhaustion, reduced capacity, emotional blunting, impaired function. The physical dimension of burnout is acknowledged but rarely given sustained attention. For the AuDHD parent in triple-layer burnout, that omission matters. The physical dimension is not a side effect of the real burnout. In many cases it is the earliest and most persistent record of it.

The body keeps score in ways the cognitive system does not. For a parent whose interoception is already altered by autism, whose masking practices have trained them to suppress the read-out of internal states, and whose executive depletion has reduced the capacity for accurate self-monitoring, the physical signals of burnout may be the only dimension of the depletion that is not being actively filtered.

This chapter addresses the somatic reality of triple-layer burnout: what the sustained autonomic activation of the triple-layer state does to the physical body over time, why those physical signals are so frequently misattributed or missed entirely, and what a body-aware approach to recovery looks like for an AuDHD parent who may have a complex and often difficult relationship with their own physical signals.

Interoception and Why Burnout Signals Are Hard to Read

Interoception is the sense that allows the brain to register the internal state of the body. Heart rate, breath quality, hunger, fullness, pain, temperature, the feeling of tension or ease in the muscles, the state of the gut: all of these are interoceptive signals.

They feed into the conscious awareness of internal state, and they form the substrate of what most people call their felt sense of how they are doing.

Research by neuroscientist Antonio Damasio and subsequent work by A. D. Craig have established interoception as a fundamental homeostatic system, not a secondary one, with Craig's work locating interoceptive processing in the anterior insular cortex as part of the brain's representation of the physiological state of the body (Craig, 2003). The interoceptive system is not a passive receiver. It actively constructs the brain's ongoing representation of bodily state and feeds that representation into emotional processing, decision-making, and the sense of self.

For autistic people, interoceptive processing is frequently atypical. This shows up in a range of ways: altered sensitivity to internal signals, difficulty discriminating between different types of internal sensation, reduced reliability of hunger or pain signals, difficulty registering emotional states through their physical correlates. This is not universally true across the autistic population, and the direction of the difference varies between individuals. But altered interoception is a well-documented feature of the autistic profile, and it has direct implications for how burnout signals are registered and reported.

For the AuDHD parent in burnout, the interoceptive gap has two layers. The first is the baseline autistic alteration: the signals may be less salient, less accurately discriminated, or less reliably linked to conscious awareness than they would be for a neurotypical person. The second is what burnout itself does to interoception: the sustained sympathetic activation of the triple-layer state narrows the available attention and reduces the processing allocated to internal signal monitoring. The parent who is operating in a chronic threat-detection state is allocating most available processing to external monitoring. Internal signals compete poorly for attention in that state.

The result is that the body may be producing clear and consistent physical signals of burnout for months before the cognitive system registers them accurately. The jaw clenching, the gut instability, the recurrent minor illness, the muscle tension that does not resolve: these are not background events. They are the body's most persistent communication, in a channel that the burnout and the autistic profile have together made harder to read.

Physical Symptoms That Are Actually Burnout

A significant proportion of the physical complaints that AuDHD parents in burnout present to their doctors are attributed to other causes: stress, functional disorders, immune system dysfunction, perimenopausal symptoms, coincidental illness. Some of those attributions may be accurate. Many of them are accurate descriptions of the mechanism while missing the cause. The chronic stress of triple-layer burnout produces physiological effects that are real, measurable, and attributable to the sustained autonomic activation rather than to the labelled condition.

The immune disruption pattern is well established in the chronic stress literature. Sustained sympathetic nervous system activation alters immune function, reducing the effectiveness of pathogen response and increasing inflammatory activity (Segerstrom and Miller, 2004). For the parent in triple-layer burnout, this shows up as recurrent illness that seems out of proportion to exposure: colds that last longer than expected, minor injuries that take longer to heal, periodic flare-ups of conditions that have an inflammatory component.

The gastrointestinal signal is one of the most consistent physical markers of sustained autonomic activation. The gut has its own nervous system, the enteric nervous system, which communicates bidirectionally with the central nervous system and is directly affected by the state of the autonomic nervous system. In a sustained sympathetic activation state, gut motility, gut sensitivity, and gut microbiome composition are all affected. For the parent who has been reporting gut problems to their doctor for months or years, the burnout connection is frequently not the first explanation offered.

The musculoskeletal tension pattern is another consistent marker. Sustained sympathetic activation maintains the muscles of the jaw, neck, shoulders, and upper back in a low-level contraction state that over time produces pain, headaches, restricted movement, and the kind of fatigue that is not relieved by sleep because the muscles do not fully release during rest.

Skin conditions with an inflammatory or stress-responsive component, including eczema, psoriasis, rosacea, and stress-related hives, frequently flare during periods of sustained autonomic activation. These are not psychosomatic in the dismissive sense of that word. They are real physiological responses to a real physiological state.

Raymaker and colleagues documented the physical dimension of autistic burnout as a consistent feature reported across their participant sample, including fatigue, increased illness, and physical shutdowns that participants described as distinct from sleep or rest and that did not resolve with standard approaches to rest (Raymaker et al., 2020). The physical burnout is not a complication of the autistic burnout. It is a feature of it.

How Masking Suppresses Physical Signals

The masking practices that AuDHD parents developed to survive neurotypical environments do not selectively suppress only the neurological features that would attract unwanted social attention. They suppress the read-out of internal states more broadly.

The autistic adult who learned to manage their visible sensory responses in social situations also learned, often implicitly and without choosing it, to suppress the internal registration of those responses. The practice of suppressing the output trained the system to reduce the signal. Over years and decades, the pathway between internal physical state and conscious awareness can become unreliable in ways that the person does not notice because the suppression has been consistent and long-standing.

This has direct implications for physical burnout signals. The pain that would produce a visible flinch in someone who had not masked that response for years may not produce a flinch, and may not produce a clear conscious pain signal, in the adult who has spent decades training the system to suppress the output. The gut distress that would prompt another person to register I am not well and need to stop may not prompt that registration in the parent whose interoceptive channel for that signal has been trained toward suppression.

Van der Kolk's research on trauma and the body has documented the way the body holds the physiological record of states that the conscious mind has managed to suppress, regulate, or stop noticing (van der Kolk, 2014). The relevance for AuDHD burnout is not that burnout is trauma, though for some parents in some situations it may meet clinical criteria, but that the mechanism of physical signal suppression through practiced masking and the mechanism of physical signal suppression through trauma response have significant overlap. In both cases, the body is maintaining a record that the cognitive system is not fully receiving.

Chronic Pain, Fatigue, and the Burnout Connection

Two physical complaints appear with disproportionate frequency in the histories of AuDHD adults in burnout: chronic pain and chronic fatigue. Both are real, both are often attributed to separate diagnostic categories, and both have a documented relationship with sustained autonomic dysregulation that is frequently not the frame used when these symptoms are assessed.

Fibromyalgia, chronic fatigue syndrome, and their related presentations involve altered pain processing, disproportionate fatigue relative to physical activity, and a range of systemic symptoms that overlap significantly with the physical profile of sustained chronic stress. The relationship between these conditions and autonomic nervous system dysregulation is an active area of research. What is relevant here is that for the AuDHD parent who has been living with triple-layer burnout for an extended period, the physical profile they describe to their doctor may be diagnosed as a separate condition when it is also and possibly primarily the physical expression of the burnout state.

This does not mean that fibromyalgia or chronic fatigue syndrome are not real conditions that merit their own clinical attention. It means that treating those conditions in isolation, without addressing the sustained autonomic activation that is driving or maintaining the physical state, is unlikely to produce sustained improvement. The physical symptoms are signals, not separate events. They require the same source-level approach that the rest of this book applies to the cognitive and emotional dimensions of the burnout.

The Autonomic Nervous System Under Triple Depletion

Stephen Porges's polyvagal theory provides the most useful framework for understanding what is happening in the body of the AuDHD parent in triple-layer burnout (Porges, 2011). The theory describes three hierarchically organised states of the autonomic nervous system: the ventral vagal state, which supports social engagement, connection, and recovery; the sympathetic state, which mobilises for threat; and the dorsal vagal state, which immobilises when threat is sustained and escape is not available.

In a well-functioning system with adequate recovery, the person moves between these states in response to actual environmental conditions, returning to ventral vagal engagement after periods of sympathetic activation. In triple-layer burnout, that return to ventral vagal is impaired. The autistic burnout has lowered the threshold at which the sympathetic system activates. The ADHD depletion has removed many of the executive strategies that were providing top-down regulation of the arousal state. The PDA parenting exhaustion has maintained a sustained high-demand relational environment that provides frequent activating stimuli without adequate recovery windows.

The body in this state is running a sustained sympathetic activation that it cannot reliably exit. Over time, the persistent sympathetic state triggers the beginning of dorsal vagal immobilisation features alongside the sympathetic activation: the flat affect, the physical shutdown responses, the sense of going through the motions without being present, the disconnection from the body's own signals that looks, from the outside, like the person is simply very tired.

Learning to Read Your Body's Burnout Signals

Because the interoceptive channel is unreliable in this profile, learning to read the body's burnout signals requires externalising the process that typically runs internally. It requires treating the body's output as data to be tracked rather than as a signal that will be automatically registered.

The most effective approach for most AuDHD parents in burnout is a brief, structured daily check-in that asks specific questions about specific physical domains rather than a global question about how you are feeling. Global questions are harder to answer accurately when interoception is unreliable because they require the integration of multiple signals into an overall assessment, which is exactly the kind of processing that is impaired. Specific questions about specific domains produce more reliable data: jaw tension at the moment of checking, gut state at the moment of checking, shoulder and neck tension at the moment of checking, quality of sleep over the previous night, presence or absence of headache.

The Burnout Early Warning Signs Tracker in Appendix D provides a format for this kind of daily tracking that is designed to take under two minutes and to be repeatable over time. The value of tracking is not just the daily data point. It is the pattern it reveals over weeks and months, which the unreliable internal monitoring system would not otherwise produce. For many parents, the first time they track their physical signals consistently for six weeks is the first time they can see clearly how long the burnout has been building, and how consistent the physical signals have been while the cognitive recognition was lagging behind them.

Physical Recovery Work for Sensory Differences

Standard physical recovery recommendations, including yoga, progressive muscle relaxation, breathing exercises, and mindfulness body scans, are designed for a nervous system that will respond to those inputs by moving toward regulation. For the AuDHD parent, those inputs produce highly variable results, and for some parents they produce the opposite of what is intended.

Yoga and progressive muscle relaxation both involve sustained attention to the physical body. For parents with interoceptive alterations, that sustained attention to the body may produce confusion, discomfort, or the anxiety of being unable to locate the sensation being targeted. For parents with sensory processing differences, the close-body awareness that these practices require may be intrusive rather than calming.

Breathing exercises have a more reliable track record for autonomic regulation across different populations, but the specific instruction and the specific technique matter. Slow exhalation relative to inhalation is the most reliably effective technique for activating the parasympathetic response, and it can often be implemented without requiring the sustained internal body attention that other somatic approaches demand. Box breathing, the physiological sigh, and low-and-slow nasal breathing are all accessible techniques that work primarily through respiratory physiology rather than through the interoceptive channel, making them more reliably effective for parents with interoceptive differences.

Physical movement that provides proprioceptive input, particularly rhythmic whole-body movement such as walking, swimming, rocking, or gentle bouncing, activates the vestibular and proprioceptive systems in ways that tend to support autonomic regulation across sensory profiles. The regulatory effect of rhythmic movement is not dependent on interoception. It works through a different channel and is therefore a more reliable entry point for the AuDHD parent whose interoceptive channel is unreliable.

Here is how the body-signal recognition process worked for one parent.

Consider Elowen (name changed), a woman in her early forties with AuDHD who had been parenting her PDA-profile daughter for eight years. Elowen had been reporting jaw pain, gut instability, and recurrent skin flares to her doctor for approximately three years. She had received treatment for each symptom separately: a dental night guard for the jaw clenching, dietary advice for the gut issues, a topical treatment for the skin condition. None of the treatments had produced consistent improvement. The symptoms would reduce for a period and then return, often together and often at times she could not predict. When Elowen began tracking her physical symptoms alongside the burnout signal clusters from Chapter 2.0, the pattern that emerged over six weeks was clear. The jaw clenching, gut instability, and skin flares were not occurring randomly. They were clustering in the weeks following extended periods of high parenting demand, with a consistent lag of approximately five to seven days between the peak of the parenting demand and the onset of the physical symptoms. Her body had been reporting the burnout peaks accurately and consistently for years. The cognitive recognition had not been available to receive that report. When she shared the tracking data with her doctor, it changed the frame of the consultation from individual symptoms to sustained autonomic activation and what to do about the source rather than the outputs. That change of frame was the beginning of a more effective approach.

What This Chapter Has Named

The physical body is not a separate record from the burnout. It is often the earliest and most persistent record of it, in a parent whose cognitive recognition system has been impaired by the same burnout it is trying to register.

Interoceptive alterations in autism, compounded by the suppressive effects of long-term masking, mean that the body's burnout signals frequently arrive before the cognitive recognition does and go unreceived for longer than they should. Physical symptoms attributed to separate diagnostic categories, including immune disruption, gastrointestinal instability, chronic pain, fatigue, and inflammatory skin conditions, are frequently the physical expression of sustained autonomic activation rather than separate events.

Learning to read the body's burnout signals requires an externalised tracking approach rather than reliance on the unreliable internal monitoring system. Physical recovery work for this profile is most effective when it bypasses the interoceptive channel rather than depending on it: rhythmic proprioceptive movement, slow exhalation breathing techniques, and sensory-calibrated approaches rather than generic mindfulness or progressive relaxation.

The body has been keeping an accurate record. The work of this chapter is learning to read it.

Chapter 5.0 Dropping the Non-Negotiable

The Addition Problem in Burnout Recovery

Almost every burnout recovery framework, at some point, tells you to add something. Add rest. Add self-care. Add time alone. Add professional support. Add better nutrition, more exercise, a therapy appointment, a mindfulness practice, a morning routine, a connection ritual with your partner. The advice is well-intentioned. It is also, for the AuDHD parent in triple-layer burnout, categorically the wrong place to start.

The addition model of burnout recovery assumes that the depleted system has room for additions. It assumes a kind of negative space that better inputs can fill. But the AuDHD parent in triple-layer burnout is not running at sixty percent capacity, leaving room for better choices to bring them back to full. They are running at or below their minimum functional threshold, with demands that continue to arrive at the same rate regardless of the internal state of the person receiving them. Adding things to a system that has no room for additions does not restore the system. It accelerates the collapse.

Before anything can be added, something has to be removed. This is not a popular truth in burnout recovery spaces, because removal is harder than addition. It requires confronting the list of things you are currently doing and deciding which of them can stop, or reduce, or be done by someone else, or not be done at all. For the AuDHD parent, that confrontation is particularly hard, because many of the items on the list feel non-negotiable. They feel fixed. They feel like things that would fall apart if they were removed.

This chapter is about discovering that most of them are not.

What Actually Has to Happen Before Anything Else

Before restoration can begin, the demand load has to reduce to a level the depleted system can sustain without continued net depletion. This is not a preference or a recommendation. It is a structural requirement. Recovery from burnout is not possible while the conditions that caused the burnout are continuing unchanged at full force.

The specific threshold varies between people and between periods. What matters is not the precise number but the direction: the daily demand load has to become something the system can handle at its current depleted level without depleting further. Not restoring, necessarily. Not thriving. Simply not getting worse. That is the first target, and it requires reduction before anything else.

For the AuDHD parent, this reduction is complicated by three specific features of their situation. First, the ADHD executive depletion has specifically impaired the internal discernment capacity that would normally distinguish urgent from non-urgent, fixed from flexible, essential from habitual. The system that would perform that triage is the system that is most depleted. Second, the autistic nervous system in burnout experiences all demands as high-cost, which means the normal priority-sorting that would identify what to drop is not available in its usual form. Third, the PDA household is generating ongoing demand that cannot simply be negotiated away. The child's needs are real, and a significant portion of the parenting demand is genuinely non-negotiable.

The audit that follows is designed to replace the internal discernment capacity that burnout has temporarily removed with an external structured process. It does not require the depleted system to accurately assess its own situation in real time. It asks a set of specific questions about a list of specific items, one at a time, and sorts the results into categories.

The Non-Negotiable Audit

The audit begins with a complete inventory. Not a mental list. An actual written list, because the working memory depletion of ADHD burnout means that anything held in memory rather than written down is unreliable. The list contains every regular demand the parent is currently meeting or attempting to meet: every obligation, task, commitment, standard, expectation, and role. Not the dramatic ones. All of them, including the ones so habitual they barely register as demands at all.

Once the list exists, each item goes through three questions.

The first question: if this item did not happen this week, would there be a direct, concrete, irreversible consequence? Not an uncomfortable consequence, not a social consequence, not the feeling that things had slipped. An irreversible concrete one. A bill that would not be paid and a service that would be cut off. A medication that would run out. A child who would not eat. The bar for yes on this question is high. Most items do not meet it.

The second question: is this item on the list because it has to be, or because I have always done it, because I agreed to it before burnout, because I would feel guilty if it did not happen, because someone else expects it, or because stopping it would require a conversation I do not currently have the resource to have? This question exposes the category that most parents find the largest on their list: things that feel fixed because of history, expectation, or the cost of renegotiation, rather than because of actual structural necessity.

The third question: if I could not do this item for six months due to a medical event, what would actually happen? This question bypasses the guilt and the expectation and the internal rules and tests the actual structural necessity of the item. Most AuDHD parents find, when they apply this question honestly, that the majority of items that felt non-negotiable in the first question reveal considerable flexibility in the third.

The categories the audit produces are: genuinely non-negotiable (cannot be safely removed without irreversible consequence), reducible (can be done at a lower standard, less frequently, or in a reduced form), delegatable (can be done by someone else, even imperfectly), deferrable (can be paused for a defined period without irreversible consequence), and removable (can be stopped, and the only consequence is discomfort, guilt, or someone else's disappointment). The recovery work starts with the removable category and works back toward the genuinely non-negotiable.

Social Obligations in Burnout: Real Cost Accounting

Social obligations have a particular relationship with the non-negotiable category in the AuDHD parent's list. They are often classified as non-negotiable not because of structural necessity but because the social cost of renegotiating them feels higher than the physiological cost of continuing to meet them. In burnout, this calculation is wrong. The physiological cost is higher than it appears to be because the masked performance of the social obligation is concealing how much it is actually costing.

Solanto's work on cognitive-behavioural approaches to ADHD has documented the role that social performance demands play in ADHD executive depletion, noting that obligations requiring sustained social performance, including meetings, social events, family gatherings, and group activities, carry a consistently higher executive function cost than their surface-level time commitment suggests (Solanto, 2011). For the autistic parent who is also masking during those events, that cost is substantially higher than the ADHD cost alone.

The real cost accounting for social obligations in burnout looks different from the standard calculation. The standard calculation counts the time. The real cost accounting counts the preparation cost (the anticipatory anxiety and planning that precedes the event), the performance cost (the masking and social regulation effort during the event), and the recovery cost (the time after the event during which the parent is depleted beyond their already depleted baseline). For many AuDHD parents, a two-hour social event costs four to six hours of total functioning capacity when preparation and recovery are included.

When this real cost is applied to the social obligations on the audit list, items that seemed manageable in terms of time frequently become clearly unsustainable in terms of actual resource. The birthday party, the workplace social event, the family gathering, the regular commitment that has been running for years: these items often move from the non-negotiable category into the reducible or deferrable category when their actual cost is accurately calculated.

Household Standards and the Good Enough Threshold

The household standards category is where many AuDHD parents find the most unexpected negotiability. The internal rules governing what a household should look like, how clean it should be, how organised, how well-fed, how structured, these rules are often experienced as objective standards rather than as choices. They feel non-negotiable in the same way that gravity feels non-negotiable. They are simply what you do.

They are not. They are standards derived from a combination of cultural exposure, family of origin patterns, personal preference, and the internal rules that the AuDHD nervous system generates to maintain the sense of control and predictability that it requires to function. Many of them were set when the parent was functioning at a higher capacity than they are now, or were set to meet someone else's expectations rather than their own.

Kristin Neff's research on self-compassion has documented the relationship between internal standards and self-criticism, finding that the person who treats themselves with the same compassion they would offer a friend in the same situation not only reports higher wellbeing but shows reduced activation of the physiological stress response under conditions of failure (Neff,

2011). For the AuDHD parent in burnout who is holding themselves to standards they cannot currently meet, the gap between the standard and the actual performance is not just distressing. It is generating a self-critical response that is itself a physiological cost on the already depleted system.

The good enough threshold is not a lower standard. It is a realistic standard for current conditions. The question is not what this household should look like when I am functioning at full capacity, but what does this household need to look like for the people in it to be safe, reasonably comfortable, and not in crisis. That threshold is almost always lower than the internal standard the burnout parent is trying to meet. The gap between the internal standard and the good enough threshold is recoverable energy that is currently being spent on a performance that is not required by the actual conditions.

Professional and Workplace Accommodation During Burnout

The professional category is where the audit most frequently stalls. Work feels non-negotiable in a way that social obligations and household standards do not, because the financial and professional consequences of reducing professional output are more concrete. For many families, they are genuinely fixed. But within the genuinely fixed professional commitments, there is almost always more flexibility than the burnout parent has allowed themselves to identify.

Barkley's extensive work on ADHD and workplace functioning has documented how ADHD executive function difficulties interact with workplace demand, noting that the ADHD employee who is operating without adequate accommodation is typically working significantly harder than their neurotypical colleagues to produce equivalent output, which over time produces the kind of accelerated depletion visible in the audit (Barkley, 2012). The parent who feels they cannot reduce their professional output because it is already at the minimum is often missing the fact that the effort required to produce that output is not the same as the effort a neurotypical colleague would require for the same task.

The accommodation question for the professional category is not: can I work less? It is: can I work in a way that costs less per unit of output? This may involve formal workplace accommodation requests, which in many jurisdictions are supported by neurodevelopmental diagnoses. It may involve reducing the social and communication overhead that surrounds the work rather than the work itself. It may involve restructuring the workday to reduce transition costs, since transitions are high-cost executive operations for the ADHD nervous system. It may involve being honest with a manager about a temporary reduction in capacity without disclosing the full clinical picture.

The professional category is the one where the audit is most likely to require a conversation the parent does not currently have the resource to have. For that reason, the professional items that cannot be immediately reduced should be identified but not addressed in the first week of the audit. The audit works from the easily removable toward the more structurally complex. Professional accommodation is in the third tier, addressed after the first two tiers have reduced the overall demand load to a level where more complex conversations become possible.

What to Say and What Not to Explain

The audit produces a list of reductions, removals, and deferrals that will require communication to people who have current expectations of the parent. The communication cost of those conversations is real, and it is worth addressing directly.

The default approach for most AuDHD parents is to over-explain. The combination of the directness of the AuDHD communication style and the internalised need to justify reduced output produces lengthy explanations of the clinical situation, the burnout framework, the triple-layer model, and the evidence base for the recovery approach. Those explanations are exhausting to produce, frequently misunderstood, and rarely necessary.

The shorter approach almost always works better: I am not able to continue with this for the time being. I am dealing with a health situation that requires me to reduce my commitments. I will let you know when that changes. This is accurate, it is not dishonest, it does not require the other person to understand the AuDHD burnout picture, and it does not generate the follow-up questions that a detailed clinical explanation tends to produce.

The over-explanation trap also appears in internal justification. The parent who drops a commitment does not need to justify it to themselves at length. The audit has already done the justification work. The item is in the removable or deferrable category. That is sufficient. The self-critical loop that follows the removal, the you should be able to manage this, everyone else does, this is not a real reason to stop, loop: this is the internal rule system generating demand resistance to the reduction that the audit has identified as necessary. Recognising it as a cognitive pattern rather than an accurate assessment allows it to run without requiring compliance.

The Permission You Have Been Waiting For

Many AuDHD parents come to the audit with a specific unspoken hope: that the process will tell them they are allowed to stop some of the things they are doing. They know, at some level, that the list is too long. They have known for a while. But the internal rule system and the external expectations and the identity investment in managing everything have been generating reasons to continue every item on the list. They are looking for external permission to do what they already know needs to happen.

This is the permission: you are allowed to stop doing things that are making you worse. You are allowed to let things be imperfect. You are allowed to communicate a reduced capacity without providing a justification that meets someone else's standard of sufficient reason. You are allowed to prioritize your survival functioning over your performance functioning. You are allowed to be a parent who is managing burnout rather than a parent who is performing management of burnout while actually deteriorating.

Neff's self-compassion framework is relevant here specifically because it addresses the internal resistance to self-permission that shows up most strongly in people who hold themselves to high internal standards (Neff, 2011). The question she proposes, what would you say to a close friend who was in this situation, is not a rhetorical device. It is a genuine calibration tool. The answer reveals the gap between the compassion available for others and the compassion the parent allows themselves, and makes the internal rule system's double standard visible.

Your Minimum Viable Household

The output of the audit is a working definition of the minimum viable household: the specific set of things that actually have to happen, at their minimum adequate standard, for the people in the household to be safe and functional. Not comfortable. Not performing well. Not meeting a cultural standard. Safe and functional.

This definition is usually shorter than the parent expects. It almost always includes: the child's essential physical needs, school or learning continuity if that is functioning, the parent's essential self-maintenance, and the financial essential. It does not include most of the things that are currently occupying a significant proportion of the parent's available resource.

The minimum viable household is not a permanent state. It is the recovery baseline: the level at which the demand load is below the depletion threshold, allowing the system to begin restoring rather than continuing to deplete. As restoration occurs, items can be added back, one at a time, with explicit attention to whether the addition produces a return to depletion. The household grows back from the minimum viable state as the system's capacity grows. But it cannot grow if it never achieves the minimum viable state in the first place.

Here is how the audit worked for one parent.

Consider Fenwick (name changed), a father in his early forties with AuDHD who was parenting two children, one of whom had a PDA profile. Fenwick came to the audit convinced that his situation was genuinely different from the scenarios the framework was designed for, that his obligations were actually fixed in a way that other people's were not. He was a self-employed professional with client commitments, a school governor, a regular volunteer at his son's football club, responsible for his elderly mother's weekly shopping, the family member who organised events for his extended family, and the parent managing the PDA household. He listed twenty-two regular weekly obligations before stopping. When he applied the three audit questions to each item in turn, fourteen of the twenty-two moved into categories other than genuinely non-negotiable. Six of those fourteen were items he had classified as fixed for years without questioning the classification, including the school governor role, which turned out to have a leave of absence provision he had not known about, and three of the family organisation obligations, which, when he communicated a temporary reduction in capacity, were taken over by other family members with considerably less drama than he had anticipated. The eight genuinely non-negotiable items were manageable at his current depleted level without continued net deterioration. The fourteen negotiable items had been the difference between sustainable depletion and the accelerating collapse that had been producing the cascade pattern for the previous eight months.

What This Chapter Has Named

Before restoration can begin, the demand load has to reduce. The addition model of burnout recovery assumes available capacity

that does not exist in the triple-layer depletion state. The audit
creates the reduction that makes restoration possible.

The non-negotiable audit externalises the triage function that
ADHD depletion has impaired. Its three questions distinguish
genuinely fixed demands from demands that feel fixed because of
internal rules, historical patterns, external expectations, or the
cost of renegotiation. The categories it produces, genuinely non-
negotiable, reducible, delegatable, deferrable, and removable,
identify where the recoverable resource is and in what order to
act on it.

The minimum viable household is the first target: not a
comfortable or performing household, but a household in which
the demand load is below the depletion threshold and restoration
can begin.

You are allowed to stop doing things that are making you worse.
The permission was always yours. The audit makes it visible.

Chapter 6.0 Identity Under Burnout

What Burnout Takes Beyond the Practical

The practical dimensions of triple-layer burnout are the ones most visible and most addressed: the executive function that has stopped working, the sensory threshold that has dropped, the recovery windows that do not exist, the demands that continue to arrive beyond the system's capacity to meet them. Those dimensions are real and they require the practical interventions this book describes. But they do not account for everything the burnout takes.

For the late-diagnosed AuDHD parent, triple-layer burnout has a dimension that sits underneath the practical and is rarely named in burnout frameworks. It takes the self-concept. Not the abstract philosophical self, but the working, functional identity: the picture of who you are that you carry into every interaction, that organises your choices, that tells you what you are capable of and what you value and what kind of parent and person you are. When burnout removes the compensatory strategies and the masking and the managed performance of competence, it removes the platform on which that self-concept was standing. And what is under the platform is often, for the late-diagnosed AuDHD adult, a great deal of unfamiliar territory.

This chapter addresses the identity dimension of burnout not as a secondary effect to be resolved after the practical recovery is complete, but as a component of the burnout itself that has to be named and engaged with directly. It is honest about the timing: in the acute burnout phase, the identity disruption is a crisis, and calling it an opportunity is too simple. But it is also honest about what the crisis opens: the possibility of an identity that does not depend on performance, that does not require the maintenance of compensatory strategies to sustain it, and that is available to the parent even at the bottom of the burnout, without the masks that burnout has taken from them.

The Mask Goes First: Identity Without Compensatory Strategies

The compensatory strategies that late-diagnosed AuDHD adults develop are not trivial. They represent decades of effortful learning, of figuring out what neurotypical functioning looks like and developing the skills to produce a version of it that is adequate for survival in neurotypical contexts. Lists and systems for the executive function deficits. Scripts and preparation for social interactions. Routines for managing sensory processing. The carefully maintained impression of someone who is managing competently, even when the effort required to maintain that impression is substantial.

These strategies serve a function beyond the practical one. They form a layer of identity. The person who has learned to manage their AuDHD through extensive compensatory scaffolding often identifies as a person who manages. The management capacity, effortful and exhausting as it is, becomes part of the self-concept: I am someone who figures things out, who meets their commitments, who copes. This identity is not a lie. The coping is real. But it is built on top of the compensatory strategies, and the compensatory strategies are built on top of the executive function and masking resources that burnout specifically depletes.

Cage and Troxell-Whitman's research on masking has documented how the compensatory strategies and masking behaviours of autistic adults become integrated into their sense of self, such that the removal of those strategies through burnout or other circumstances is experienced as an identity loss rather than simply a functional loss (Cage and Troxell-Whitman, 2019). This integration makes the burnout's identity dimension more acute than it would be for someone whose sense of self did not depend on the continued availability of the strategies that burnout removes.

When the burnout arrives and the compensatory strategies fail, the late-diagnosed AuDHD parent is left with a self-concept that has lost its structural support. The list systems that were organising the ADHD are not working. The social scripts that were managing the interactions are failing mid-execution. The routines that were protecting the sensory system are not accessible. The performance of competence that was producing the identity of a person who manages is no longer possible to sustain. What is left is not nothing. But it is unfamiliar, and it is available to the parent at the moment when they have the least resource to explore it.

Late Diagnosis and the Burnout Identity Crisis

For the AuDHD parent who received their diagnosis in adulthood, the identity dimension of burnout carries an additional layer. Late diagnosis does not simply add a new piece of information to an existing self-concept. It reorganises the retrospective account of the life that came before it.

The experiences that were previously attributed to character flaws or personal inadequacy, the struggles at school that produced the sense of being less capable than expected, the relationship difficulties attributed to social awkwardness or emotional immaturity, the career difficulties attributed to laziness or poor follow-through, the parenting difficulties attributed to inadequate effort or wrong choices, these experiences are reinterpreted through the lens of the neurodevelopmental profile. The reorganisation is often experienced as clarifying and even relieving. But it is also, for many late-diagnosed AuDHD adults, profoundly disorienting.

Leedham and colleagues' research on the late diagnosis experience found that late-diagnosed autistic adults frequently reported a period of identity reconstruction following diagnosis, in which the prior self-concept, which had been constructed without accurate knowledge of the neurodevelopmental profile, was no longer coherent, and a new self-concept had not yet been built (Leedham et al., 2020). For the AuDHD parent who is in the middle of this reconstruction process when the burnout arrives,

the two disruptions compound each other. The burnout removes
the compensatory strategies at the same moment that the late
diagnosis has called into question the self-concept those
strategies were supporting.

The timing is not coincidental. Late diagnosis frequently arrives
during or shortly before burnout, because burnout is often what
prompts the assessment in the first place. The parent who has
been managing with compensatory strategies for decades reaches
a point at which the strategies begin to fail, seeks support, and
receives a diagnosis that explains why the strategies were always
so costly and why they have begun to fail now. The diagnosis and
the burnout arrive together, and their identity implications arrive
together.

The Grief That Arrives Mid-Burnout

One of the most consistently underacknowledged features of the
late-diagnosed AuDHD burnout experience is grief. Not grief for
a single loss, but a compound grief with multiple objects: grief
for the easier life that would have been possible with earlier
diagnosis and support, grief for the years spent building and
maintaining compensatory strategies that should never have been
necessary, grief for the identity that was constructed without
accurate information about the self it was meant to describe, and
grief for the parent the AuDHD person had hoped to be before
the burnout made the gap between that hope and the current
reality impossible to ignore.

Pearson and Rose's work on autistic burnout and identity has
documented the grief process as a consistent feature of the
burnout experience for autistic adults, noting that the burnout
strips the defence mechanisms that had been keeping the grief at
bay, leaving the person with both the burnout and the
unprocessed emotional material that the compensatory work had
been managing alongside everything else (Pearson and Rose,
2021). For the AuDHD parent, this grief has a specific relational
dimension: the awareness of what the burnout is doing to the

parenting relationship, and the fear that the damage will be irreversible.

The grief is real and it deserves to be named. The tendency in burnout recovery frameworks is to move quickly past the emotional dimension toward the practical one, to identify what needs to change and build the architecture for changing it. That movement is necessary. But if it happens before the grief is acknowledged, the grief does not resolve. It compounds. The parent who is told to build recovery systems while they are also grieving the identity that the burnout has taken, the diagnosis that rewrites their history, and the parenting relationship they had hoped to have, is being asked to build in a space that has not been cleared.

The acknowledgement does not require extended therapeutic processing in the acute phase. It requires the parent to know that what they are feeling is real, that it is a genuine response to genuine loss, and that the loss does not define what comes after it.

Who You Are When You Cannot Perform Competence

This is the question that sits at the centre of the burnout identity crisis for the AuDHD parent: who are you when you cannot do the things you have always done?

The answer that the burnout produces in its acute phase is often: I do not know. And that not-knowing is frightening in proportion to how completely the performance of competence had become the answer to that question before the burnout removed it.

The parent who has been managing the household, the parenting relationship, the professional life, and the AuDHD profile through extensive compensatory scaffolding may not have had to ask who they are without the scaffolding since childhood. The scaffolding went up alongside the identity. It has been there so long that it has been mistaken for the building rather than the scaffolding. When the burnout takes the scaffolding, the question of what was supporting what becomes urgent.

What is usually underneath the scaffolding, when the parent can access it and sit with it without the noise of the performance anxiety and the self-criticism and the grief, is a set of values and responses and ways of engaging with the world that are not performance and not compensation. They are the autistic and ADHD ways of being that were never the problem, that have been partially obscured by the compensatory overlay, and that are still present at the bottom of the burnout when the overlay has fallen away.

The intensity of feeling about things that matter. The precision of interest in subjects that are genuinely interesting. The directness of communication. The commitment to honesty. The specific way of processing the world that produces both the difficulties and the advantages of the AuDHD profile. These are not the compensatory strategies. They are what the compensatory strategies were built on top of. And they do not require the compensatory strategies to exist.

Distinguishing Burnout From Permanent Change

One of the most destabilising features of the burnout identity crisis is the difficulty of knowing whether the changes in capacity and self-perception are burnout-related and therefore recoverable, or permanent and therefore requiring a fundamental revision of the self-concept going forward.

This question is not easily answered in the acute phase, and the attempt to answer it definitively in the acute phase is itself a problem. The parent who is trying to determine whether they will ever be able to do the things they could do before the burnout, while they are still in the burnout, is attempting a calibration with a broken instrument.

Pearson and Rose's research documented that autistic adults in burnout frequently reported catastrophising about permanence during the acute phase, interpreting current limitations as permanent ones, and that this catastrophising was itself a feature of the burnout rather than an accurate assessment of long-term prognosis (Pearson and Rose, 2021). The burnout alters the felt sense of what is possible in a direction that does not accurately represent what recovery will produce.

The more useful frame is not: will I recover everything I had? It is: the current state is a burnout state, not a permanent state, and burnout states have features that distinguish them from permanent changes, including their relationship to demand level, their trajectory over time with appropriate support, and their response to the specific interventions this book describes. The things that are not available in the burnout are not necessarily unavailable permanently. And some of the things that become visible in the burnout, the unfamiliar territory under the compensatory scaffolding, are not losses. They are findings.

The Parent Identity Under PDA Parenting Pressure

The parenting dimension of the burnout identity crisis deserves its own attention. The AuDHD parent who has been parenting a PDA child has been operating in a parenting context that provides consistent negative feedback on their parenting identity in ways that neurotypical parents of neurotypical children do not typically experience.

The PDA child's nervous system generates behavior that, in the absence of understanding the PDA profile, reads as a response to parenting failure. Demand avoidance, meltdowns, refusals, shutdowns, the inability to comply with even the most reasonable requests: these behaviors, when they are persistent and severe, are experienced by the parent as evidence of something they are doing wrong, even when the parent has read all the literature and understands the neurology. The felt experience of the child's persistent dysregulation is a persistent implicit feedback that the parenting is failing.

For the AuDHD parent in burnout, this implicit feedback lands on a self-concept that is already destabilised by the burnout's removal of the compensatory scaffolding. The parent who is already asking who they are without their competence performance now also has to contend with the felt sense that their most important role, the parenting role, is the one in which they are most visibly failing. The combination is specifically corrosive to the parenting identity in a way that the burnout recovery framework cannot ignore.

The corrective is not positivity. It is accuracy. The PDA child's behavior is not feedback on parenting quality in the way that behavior is in neurotypical parent-child dyads. It is the output of a nervous system in threat-detection mode, which is a feature of the child's neurology rather than a measure of the parent's performance. The parent who can access this understanding, even partially and inconsistently, has a frame for separating the child's behavior from the parenting identity that makes the identity crisis somewhat less acute.

Building an Identity That Does Not Require Performance

The longer-term work that the burnout opens, when the acute phase has reduced sufficiently for this work to be possible, is the construction of an identity that does not depend on the continued successful deployment of the compensatory strategies.

This work is not abstract. It begins with specific questions, approached at the pace the depleted system can tolerate. Not all at once. Not as a project. As an ongoing, low-demand inquiry that runs in the background of the practical recovery work.

What do you value when you are not performing valuing? What do you actually find interesting, as distinct from what you have learned to signal interest in? What parts of your way of engaging

with the world are genuinely yours, rather than compensatory
constructions over the parts you were told were inadequate?
What does care for your child look like when it comes from your
actual values rather than your performance of a parenting ideal?

Neff's self-compassion framework, which grounds self-concept in
common humanity and present-moment kindness rather than in
performance and achievement, offers a useful starting structure
for this inquiry (Neff, 2011). The self-compassionate self-concept
is not dependent on what you can do. It is grounded in what you
are, which remains accessible even at the bottom of the burnout.

Consider Godric (name changed), a father in his mid-forties who
received an AuDHD diagnosis eighteen months before the
burnout he describes as his worst period. He had been a highly
successful professional, an involved and active parent, and by his
own account a person who had never failed to manage anything
he had taken on. The burnout arrived gradually and then
suddenly: he could no longer initiate work tasks, could not
maintain the PDA parenting approach with his daughter, could
not produce the social performance that his professional role
required, and found himself, for the first time in his adult life,
with no clear answer to the question of who he was. The
professional identity had failed. The managing parent identity
had failed. What remained, when he was honest enough with
himself to look at it, was surprisingly unfamiliar. He had been
performing the professional identity and the capable parent
identity for so long that he had not noticed he had no clear sense
of what lay beneath them. The burnout, as he described it much
later, was the first time in decades he had been forced to find out.
He describes the process as the most uncomfortable thing he has
ever done, and also, eventually, as the most useful. Not because it
produced a comfortable answer to who he is, but because it
produced an honest one. The identity he has built since is smaller
than the one the burnout took. It does not require the
compensatory scaffolding. It does not perform competence. And
it has survived, so far, the ongoing difficulty of the parenting
situation he is still navigating.

What This Chapter Has Named

For the late-diagnosed AuDHD parent, triple-layer burnout includes an identity dimension that goes beyond the practical. The burnout removes the compensatory strategies that were both managing the AuDHD profile and forming the structural support for the self-concept. Without them, the question of who you are without your performance of competence becomes urgent at the worst possible moment.

The identity crisis of burnout in this profile has specific features: the late-diagnosis reorientation that may be arriving simultaneously, the grief for what the burnout has taken and what earlier diagnosis might have prevented, the difficulty distinguishing burnout-related changes from permanent ones, and the specific corrosion of the parenting identity that the PDA household's implicit feedback produces.

Burnout from the current depleted state is real. It is also, for most people in most circumstances, a burnout state rather than a permanent state. The features of the burnout, including the identity disruption, have a trajectory with appropriate support.

The longer-term opportunity is an identity that does not depend on performance. That opportunity is not accessible in the acute phase. But naming it, and naming it accurately as an opportunity rather than a consolation, changes something about how the acute phase is endured.

Chapter 7.0 Building Your Recovery Architecture

Why Willpower Cannot Be the Recovery Strategy

Every recovery approach that depends on the person in burnout making a good decision in real time will fail. Not occasionally. Consistently and predictably, because the burnout has specifically damaged the system responsible for making good decisions in real time. Asking the triple-layer depleted AuDHD parent to identify what they need, choose to access it, initiate the action, and tolerate the transition into it is asking the patient to perform surgery on themselves. The tools required for the operation are precisely the tools that are least available.

This is not a character observation. It is a neurological one. Barkley's framework for ADHD executive function documents in detail how the self-regulatory systems that govern planning, initiation, self-monitoring, and the management of internal states are the systems that ADHD depletion specifically degrades (Barkley, 2012). When those systems are depleted, the parent cannot reliably access a recovery process that requires them to work. The intention is intact. The pathway from intention to action is not. Every recovery plan that relies on daily willpower decisions will fail at the moment when the need for it is greatest, because that moment of greatest need is also the moment of deepest depletion.

The alternative is not a different kind of willpower, a better version of trying harder. The alternative is architecture: a recovery structure built into the environment and the daily pattern during a calmer window, so that it operates without requiring the depleted system to access it through deliberate choice. The architecture carries the load that willpower cannot.

Environmental Design as the Alternative

Environmental design is the arrangement of the physical and temporal environment to produce desired behaviours without requiring in-the-moment decision-making. It is the most reliable behavioural intervention for ADHD, precisely because it operates through a different channel than willpower. The person does not have to choose the behaviour in real time if the environment makes the behaviour the default.

Barkley has consistently argued that for ADHD, external scaffolding in the environment is more reliable than internal scaffolding through self-regulation, because the internal scaffolding is the site of the deficit (Barkley, 2012). The implication for recovery architecture is direct: instead of asking the depleted AuDHD parent to remember to take a recovery window, remember what recovery looks like for them specifically, initiate the transition into it, and sustain it without the executive function looping back to the undone task list, the architecture makes the recovery window happen by default. It is protected in the calendar before the rest of the day fills. The specific activity is decided in advance. The environment is arranged so that the activity has the lowest possible initiation threshold. The parent does not decide whether to do it. The decision was made during the design phase.

The environmental design principle applies across all three tiers of recovery: micro, meso, and macro. Each tier operates through different mechanisms, requires different levels of planning, and produces different types of restoration. Together they form the recovery architecture that replaces willpower as the primary delivery mechanism for recovery.

The Three Recovery Windows: Micro, Meso, Macro

The three-tier framework distinguishes between recovery windows by duration, integration with daily life, and the type of restoration they produce.

Micro-recovery windows are two to five minutes in length, integrated directly into existing daily patterns without requiring additional time. They do not require the parent to find time they do not have. They repurpose transitions, gaps, and regular pauses that already exist in the day: the two minutes after the school drop-off before starting the car, the gap between ending one work task and beginning the next, the moment before getting out of bed, the time while the kettle boils. Micro-recovery does not restore from triple-layer depletion. It prevents the ongoing accumulation of additional depletion during the day. Porges's work on vagal tone and brief autonomic recovery is relevant here: even brief periods of low-demand stimulation, in a safe context, support the maintenance of vagal tone over time and reduce the rate at which sustained activation depletes the parasympathetic reserve (Porges, 2011). Micro-recovery is the maintenance work that keeps the overall depletion from accelerating.

Meso-recovery sessions are thirty to sixty minutes in length, designed as dedicated restoration periods that occur on a predictable schedule, ideally daily or at minimum three times per week. They require protected time and a specific, pre-decided activity calibrated to the three depletion layers. These are the sessions that actually begin to restore rather than simply preventing further depletion. They are the equivalent of a charge cycle rather than simply switching off battery-intensive processes.

Macro-recovery refers to extended periods of substantially reduced demand load: days off, holiday periods, or in more acute burnout situations, periods of medical leave or significantly restructured responsibility. Macro-recovery addresses the depth of depletion that micro and meso cannot reach. It requires external support, because the parent cannot generate macro-recovery alone in a household with a PDA child's ongoing demand structure. The macro-recovery tier is the most structurally difficult to access and requires the most advance planning and external scaffolding to protect once accessed.

Building Micro-Recovery Into the Daily Flow

The first step in building micro-recovery is the existing-pattern inventory: a written list of every transition, gap, and regular pause that already occurs in the parent's day. Not the ideal day. The actual day, including the difficult periods and the chaos. The inventory typically produces more available micro-windows than the parent expects, because many of the existing gaps in the day are currently being occupied by stimulation, phone use, or background cognitive load rather than being used as recovery.

Common micro-recovery windows in the AuDHD parent's day include: the period immediately after school drop-off before any other task begins; the gap between waking and the first demand of the day; lunch breaks if the parent is working; transition moments between work tasks; the gap between the child's bedtime and the parent's own evening commitments; and the brief periods during the day when the household is momentarily settled.

Once the existing windows are identified, each one is assigned a specific micro-recovery activity and that assignment is fixed in advance. The assignment decisions are made during the design phase, not in the moment. The activity must meet three criteria: it must start immediately without initiation steps, it must be feasible in the full duration of the window even on the worst days, and it must not generate guilt or the awareness of competing obligations while in progress.

For most AuDHD parents, the most effective micro-recovery activities are: sitting in silence in a parked car after school drop-off, with the radio off and no phone; slow, deliberate nasal breathing for two minutes at a transition point; proprioceptive input through brief repetitive movement; or a thirty-second special interest contact, reading a sentence from a preferred text or looking at one image from a preferred collection.

The Meso-Recovery Session: What It Is

The meso-recovery session is the central mechanism of the recovery architecture. It is the period that, when consistently protected and correctly designed, produces the most measurable restoration across all three depletion layers.

A correctly designed meso-recovery session has the following properties. It is scheduled at the same time on the same days each week, so that it operates through habit rather than through daily decision-making. It is protected against other claims on the same time, meaning that it is treated in the calendar with the same non-negotiable status as a medical appointment. The activity used in the session has been pre-selected based on the individual's three-layer restoration profile from Chapter 3.0 and is not decided freshly each session. The activity meets all the restoration criteria for this parent's profile: below the sensory cost threshold for the autistic system, dopamine-generating for the ADHD system, and absent of the relational demand structure that drives PDA parenting exhaustion.

The most common error in building meso-recovery is making it conditional. The session that happens if everything else is done is the session that consistently does not happen. The session that happens if the child is settled is the session that is cancelled whenever the child is dysregulated, which is precisely when the session is most needed. The architecture removes conditionality from the meso-recovery session. It happens because it is on the architecture. The decision was made in advance. The depleted system is not being asked to make it again in real time.

Kessler and colleagues documented how ADHD executive function deficits specifically affect planning and follow-through for self-care and health-maintenance behaviours, finding that the gap between intending to engage in restorative behaviours and actually doing so is substantially wider for people with ADHD than for neurotypical populations, and that the most effective interventions were those that reduced the real-time decision burden (Kessler et al., 2006). The meso-recovery session's design is a direct application of that finding.

Macro-Recovery: The Longer Arc

Macro-recovery is the tier that most AuDHD parents of PDA children have not accessed, and the tier that the cascade pattern, described in Chapter 1.0, most consistently prevents. The same conditions that make macro-recovery most necessary, the deepest burnout, the most dysregulated child, the most depleted parent, are the conditions that make it most structurally difficult to arrange.

The planning principle for macro-recovery is that it must be arranged during a less acute period, for use during a more acute period, with external support already in place before it is needed. The parent who attempts to arrange extended recovery when they are at the bottom of the cascade is attempting to build infrastructure with no available tools. The parent who builds the infrastructure during a calmer period has it available when the acute period arrives.

Raymaker and colleagues identified environmental factors, including access to adequate time off and reduced demand environments, as among the most significant predictors of recovery from autistic burnout, noting that participants who had access to extended periods of reduced demand showed substantially better outcomes than those who attempted to recover while maintaining full demand load (Raymaker et al., 2020). The research finding is not surprising. The challenge is structural: for the PDA parenting household, reduced demand environments for the parent do not arise naturally. They have to be built, in advance, with external scaffolding.

The external scaffolding required for macro-recovery includes: a named person or group of people who can take over the primary household and parenting responsibility during the macro-recovery period, arrangements made and tested before they are urgently needed, the parent's minimum viable household framework already defined so that the person covering knows exactly what is essential and what can drop, and the parent's explicit permission, given to themselves in advance, to actually use the recovery period for recovery rather than for catching up on everything that has accumulated.

Recovery Infrastructure for the PDA Household

The PDA household has specific features that require adjustments to the standard recovery architecture. The child's nervous system is the primary demand generator in the household, and it does not accommodate scheduled recovery windows in the way that neurotypical children might. The adjustments that make the architecture workable in this specific context are not compromises. They are specifications.

Micro-recovery windows in the PDA household must be timed to the child's patterns rather than to an external schedule. If the child is reliably more settled in the early morning before demand has accumulated, the micro-recovery is positioned there. If the child is reliably more settled in the hour after school when they are decompressing in their room, that hour contains the micro-recovery window. The architecture is built around the actual household rhythm rather than the ideal one.

Meso-recovery in the PDA household typically requires the child to be physically elsewhere, asleep, or in a period of independent settled engagement that does not require the parent's active monitoring. The most reliable meso-recovery windows in PDA households are found during school hours if the parent is not working, during the child's own special interest engagement periods when the parent's presence is not required, and during co-parenting windows if a second parent or trusted adult is present. The architecture maps these windows before they are needed and protects them consistently.

One additional consideration for the PDA household is the parent's own demand-avoidant features. The architecture that is itself experienced as a demand, as something the parent has to do, will be avoided with the same automatic nervous system response that the child shows to external demands. The architecture has to be framed, as much as possible, as something the parent wants to do rather than something they are required to do. This is less about language and more about genuinely designing the recovery sessions around activities the parent actually finds restorative, rather than activities they think they should find restorative.

What to Automate, Reduce, and Protect

The architecture has three operational modes: automation, reduction, and protection.

Automation applies to the aspects of the household and daily functioning that currently require active decision-making but do not need to. Meals that are on a rotation rather than decided daily. Standing orders and automatic payments that remove the executive function cost of remembering regular bills. Default answers to regular communication requests rather than fresh responses each time. The objective of automation is to reduce the number of active decisions the depleted executive function system has to make each day, reserving its limited resources for the things that actually require real-time decision-making.

Reduction applies to the demand items that survived the Chapter 5.0 audit but can still be done at a lower standard or with less cognitive overhead than they are currently. The dinner that is adequate rather than nutritionally optimal. The communication response that is shorter than the depleted parent would prefer to write. The household standard that is good enough rather than good. Reduction is ongoing, not a one-time event. Each week's minimum viable operation is evaluated against the current capacity level, and the standards applied are calibrated to what is actually available.

Protection applies specifically to the recovery windows. The micro, meso, and macro windows are protected from the same categories of demand that consumed them before the architecture was built: the urgent request that could wait, the task that feels

important because it is visible, the social obligation that generates
guilt when declined. Protection is the active component of the
architecture, and it is the component most likely to erode if the
architecture is not treated as non-negotiable. The calendar
protection is the minimum. The internal permission to maintain
it, even when the erosion pressure increases, is the ongoing work.

The Recovery Architecture Blueprint

The blueprint is a single document that makes the architecture
explicit and portable. It is designed to be readable by another
adult in the event that the parent reaches a point at which they
cannot verbally communicate their needs. It contains four
sections.

The first section is the micro-recovery map: every identified
micro-window in the day, the specific activity assigned to each,
and the conditions under which each window is most reliably
available.

The second section is the meso-recovery schedule: the specific
days and times of the protected meso-recovery sessions, the
activity or activities used in them, and the name of the person
responsible for maintaining the household during each session.

The third section is the macro-recovery plan: the names and
contact details of the people who form the macro-recovery
support network, the specific responsibilities each person covers
during a macro-recovery period, and the minimum viable
household definition that guides them.

The fourth section is the early warning indicators: the physical
and functional signals from the Chapter 2.0 and Chapter 4.0 work
that indicate the burnout is deepening and the architecture needs
to be activated at a higher tier. These indicators allow the parent
or their support network to identify when micro and meso are
insufficient and macro-recovery is required, before the cascade

has progressed to the point where arranging macro-recovery is impossible.

Here is how one parent built and used this architecture.

Consider Hadrian (name changed), a parent in his early forties with AuDHD whose son had a PDA profile. Hadrian had been aware for several months that he needed to do something different about his recovery but had been unable to identify what or to access it when he thought he knew. The pattern was consistent: he would identify a recovery activity, attempt it, and find that by the time he reached the identified window the executive function required to initiate it had been consumed by the preceding demands of the day. When he worked with the architecture framework, the insight that changed the approach was identifying what already existed rather than what he planned to create. The school drop-off each morning produced a twenty-minute window of silence in the car before Hadrian began his workday. He had been using that window to make phone calls, listen to podcasts, and process the day's email backlog. The window was already there. It had been occupied by demand rather than recovery. He changed a single thing: for six weeks, the twenty minutes after drop-off were silence. No calls. No podcast. No email. The car sat in a car park near the school and Hadrian did nothing. At the end of six weeks, the measurable change in his baseline functional level was more significant than anything he had achieved in the preceding year of attempting deliberate recovery interventions. The architecture required no additional time. It required the protection of time that already existed. The recovery happened because the environment was changed to produce it, not because Hadrian made a better decision in real time on any given morning.

What This Chapter Has Named

Recovery for the AuDHD parent in triple-layer burnout cannot depend on willpower or real-time good decision-making, because burnout specifically degrades those capacities. The recovery architecture replaces willpower with environmental design: a structure built during a calmer window and operated by habit and protection rather than by daily deliberate choice.

The three-tier framework matches recovery windows to what is actually available. Micro-recovery prevents accelerating depletion through two-to-five minute interventions integrated into existing daily patterns. Meso-recovery begins actual restoration through protected, pre-designed thirty-to-sixty minute sessions. Macro-recovery addresses deep depletion through extended reduced-demand periods that require external support and advance planning.

The architecture blueprint makes the whole system explicit and portable. It does not depend on the depleted parent to hold it in memory or execute it through willpower. It depends on the environment to deliver it.

Chapter 8.0 The Support Question

The Support Problem in This Specific Context

Most burned-out people are told to reach out. Connect with others. Accept help when it is offered. Let people in. This advice is not wrong in principle. But for the AuDHD parent of a PDA child, it is delivered without the essential second half: reach out to the right people, in the right way, for the right things. Without that second half, the reach-out produces a specific kind of disappointment that is worse than not reaching out, because it consumes the limited resource of the attempt and returns advice that does not fit, practical help that creates new problems, and the isolating feeling that even the people who care about you do not understand.

The support problem in this specific context is a mismatch problem. The frameworks from which most support is offered, including professional support, well-meaning family, friends with parenting experience, and mainstream parenting communities, do not include the intersection of AuDHD parenting and PDA. The person who tells you to set clearer limits is working from a framework that does not include the PDA nervous system. The person who tells you to take some time for yourself is working from a framework that does not include the PDA household's structural resistance to recovery windows. The therapist who suggests that you explore the feelings underlying the conflict is working from a framework that may not include either the autistic communication profile or the PDA child's specific relational dynamics. The help is genuinely intended. The framework is wrong. The mismatch produces advice that cannot be implemented in the actual household, and the parent is left feeling not only unsupported but subtly blamed for their inability to implement it.

This chapter is about identifying what support actually looks like in this specific context and building toward it rather than toward the generic support frameworks that will consistently underdeliver.

Why Neurotypical Support Often Makes Things Worse

The double empathy problem, first articulated by Damian Milton, describes the bidirectional mismatch between autistic and neurotypical social cognition: the difficulty is not a deficit in autistic social processing but a genuine difference between two cognitive profiles that makes mutual understanding effortful in both directions (Milton, 2012). The communication and support mismatch experienced by AuDHD parents in burnout is a specific application of this broader principle.

When the AuDHD parent in burnout describes their experience to a neurotypical support person, several things happen that reduce the quality of the support. The communication style of the AuDHD parent, which is typically more direct, more literal, and more focused on specific details than neurotypical communication, may be read as complaint, catastrophising, or a request for practical problem-solving when it is actually a need for specific understanding. The neurotypical support person's response, which is calibrated to neurotypical distress communication, will typically involve reframing, problem-solving, or normalising, none of which address what the AuDHD parent actually communicated or needed.

The specific content of the AuDHD burnout experience is also frequently misunderstood by neurotypical support. The description of sensory overload in the household is heard as hypersensitivity that could be managed with attitude adjustment. The description of the PDA child's behavior is heard as a parenting challenge to be solved with a different strategy. The description of ADHD executive collapse is heard as a motivation problem. Each of these misreadings produces advice that is not only unhelpful but generates the secondary cost of the parent having to manage the support person's misunderstanding, explaining why the advice does not apply, and navigating the implicit suggestion that the difficulty is partly of their own making.

What Useful Support Actually Looks Like

Useful support for the AuDHD parent of a PDA child in burnout has a specific profile. It is practical rather than advisory. It does not generate additional demands. It does not require explanation or justification. It is repeatable and predictable rather than offered once and withdrawn when the need persists.

The most consistently useful support is operational: the specific task done, the specific hour covered, the specific responsibility removed. It is not the general offer to help if you need anything, which requires the depleted parent to identify a need, formulate a request, and make contact. It is the standing arrangement: I will collect the children on Tuesdays. The shopping will be delivered on Thursdays. I will be there at 7pm on Fridays so you can be elsewhere. The useful support is specific, recurring, and does not require the depleted parent to initiate it each time.

The second form of useful support is witness. Not advice. Not reframing. Not the positive perspective. Witness is the explicit acknowledgement that what the parent is experiencing is real, that it is hard, and that the difficulty makes sense given the actual conditions. For the AuDHD parent who has been managing a significant proportion of the difficulty invisibly, often without the people closest to them having an accurate picture of what the household actually requires, witness is both rare and disproportionately restorative. It does not fix anything. It changes the isolation, and isolation is itself a significant physiological cost on the depleted system.

The third form of useful support is understanding without explanation required. The support person who has done their own reading about AuDHD and PDA, who has a working framework for what the household actually contains, reduces the cognitive load of every support interaction by removing the need for the parent to translate their experience into neurotypical terms before it can be received.

Identifying Your Actual Support Network

The most important step in building adequate support is separating what exists from what should exist. Most AuDHD parents in burnout have a mental map of their support network that includes people who are emotionally invested in their wellbeing but who, on honest examination, are not providing support that actually helps. They also have relationships that they have not classified as support, which on examination are providing more consistent practical assistance or genuine understanding than the officially classified network.

Shepherd and colleagues' research on parental stress and support networks found that the quantity of support relationships was a significantly weaker predictor of wellbeing than the quality of the support received within those relationships, and that parents who had one or two relationships providing specific, practical, and emotionally attuned support showed better outcomes than parents with larger networks of lower-quality support (Shepherd et al., 2018). For the AuDHD parent in burnout, the audit of the support network is as important as the audit of obligations from Chapter 5.0.

The support audit asks three questions for each person in the parent's network. First: after contact with this person, do I typically feel better or worse than before? Second: does this person provide support that I can actually use in my actual household, or support that I would need a different household to benefit from? Third: does this person require me to manage their emotional response to my situation, or are they able to receive an honest account of my experience without generating a response I then have to manage?

The audit typically reveals that the most reliable sources of actual support are not always the most emotionally significant relationships. The sister who provides weekly practical help may be more genuinely supportive in recovery terms than the close friend whose emotional investment produces worry, advice, and the need to reassure her that you are managing. The online community of AuDHD parents may be providing more relevant witness and understanding than any local in-person network. The audit makes these realities visible so that the parent can allocate the limited resource of social contact toward the relationships that actually restore rather than the relationships that carry the most emotional expectation.

The Isolation of the AuDHD Parenting Experience

The isolation that many AuDHD parents of PDA children report is not simply a function of having limited social contact. It is the specific isolation of an experience that is not understood, not reflected in mainstream parenting culture, and not validated by the professional systems that should be most equipped to understand it.

Neff's work on self-compassion has documented the role of perceived isolation, the sense of being uniquely afflicted while others manage well, as a significant amplifier of distress and a barrier to self-compassion (Neff, 2011). For the AuDHD parent whose household is genuinely atypical by the standards of most parenting frameworks they encounter, the perceived isolation reflects a real difference rather than a cognitive distortion. The correction is not to challenge the perception but to find the communities and relationships in which the experience is shared and understood.

The specific community of AuDHD parents of PDA children is a small but real and currently growing population within the broader neurodivergent parenting community. The parents in that community are the ones most likely to receive an accurate description of the household, respond with recognition rather than reframing, and offer practical wisdom drawn from direct experience of the same specific configuration. The value of that kind of peer support, for the isolated AuDHD parent in burnout, is not supplementary to other support. For many parents, it is the primary source of genuine support available.

Professional Support: What to Look For and Avoid

Professional support has the potential to be the most structurally significant element of the recovery support network. A therapist or counsellor who understands AuDHD burnout, PDA, and the specific demands of this household can provide a consistent regulated presence, a framework for the recovery work, and clinical skills that peer support cannot replicate. The same professional in the wrong framework can actively impede recovery by applying the wrong model, generating advice that cannot be implemented in the actual household, and producing the specific injury of expert-confirmed misunderstanding.

The most important criterion for professional support selection is framework compatibility. The therapist who works primarily from attachment theory will bring useful skills but will need to understand that the attachment dynamics in the PDA household do not follow standard patterns. The therapist who works from a CBT framework will need to understand that the executive function required to implement standard CBT homework is one of the systems most depleted by ADHD burnout. The therapist who uses the language of emotional regulation without awareness of autistic interoceptive differences may be targeting a capacity that is not functioning in the way they assume.

The questions that reveal framework compatibility in an initial consultation include: how do you approach working with autistic adults? Do you have experience with PDA? How do you adapt your approach when executive function difficulties make standard homework assignments unfeasible? What is your understanding of the relationship between autistic burnout and standard burnout? A practitioner who responds to these questions with curiosity and adaptation is likely to be more useful than one who responds with confidence in a framework that does not include these variables.

What to avoid in professional support is a shorter list: avoid practitioners who respond to descriptions of the AuDHD experience with diagnostic disagreement, who attribute PDA behavior primarily to parenting choices, who suggest that the autism or ADHD diagnosis is secondary to emotional or psychological factors, or who generate additional demand through homework, structured exercises, or regular contact requirements at a rate the depleted system cannot sustain.

Online and Community Support: Real Value and Limitations

Online communities of AuDHD parents, and specifically communities focused on PDA parenting, have become a significant source of support for the isolated parents in this specific configuration. The value of these communities is real and in some cases primary: they provide the understanding without explanation, the witness from peers who share the same experience, the practical wisdom that comes from lived knowledge rather than clinical distance.

Research on neurodivergent peer support demonstrates the unique value of shared lived experience in recovery processes. Crompton et al.'s groundbreaking work on peer support has documented how neurodivergent-to-neurodivergent information transfer is significantly more effective than traditional neurotypical-led interventions, with their 2020 study showing that "autistic peer-to-peer information transfer is highly effective" in ways that differ fundamentally from neurotypical communication patterns (Crompton et al., 2020). Subsequent research on neurodivergent peer support programs found that these connections provide "safe spaces within schools for making friendships" and opportunities to "learn about neurodiversity, explore their feelings relating to their own neurodivergence" - forms of validation and identity affirmation that mainstream educational and clinical support systems typically fail to provide

(Crompton et al., 2024). For populations whose lived experience diverges significantly from neurotypical norms, peer relationships offer irreplaceable benefits including reduced isolation, increased self-acceptance, and the development of positive neurodivergent identity, which correlates directly with better mental health outcomes (Fotheringham et al., 2023).

The limitations of online community support are also real. Communities require active participation to provide support, which requires the executive function and social energy that burnout has specifically depleted. Communities can expose the parent to others' acute distress at a rate that increases rather than decreases the overall distress load, particularly for the autistic parent who absorbs emotional content from their environment more readily than neurotypical people typically do. Communities can generate implicit comparison with parents who are managing better or worse, which is rarely useful. The parent who uses online community support as their only support form may find that it provides witness and validation but not the practical operational help that reduces the actual demand load.

The most effective use of online community support is as a complement to practical support rather than a substitute for it: a source of understanding, validation, and practical wisdom from peers, combined with at least one other support form that addresses the operational demands of the household.

How to Ask When You Do Not Know What You Need

One of the specific difficulties of asking for support in triple-layer burnout is that the burnout has impaired the interoceptive and self-monitoring systems that would normally identify what is needed. The parent who cannot accurately read their own internal state cannot produce an accurate support request. They know they are not managing. They do not know what would help. And the executive depletion means that producing a support request at all requires resources that are not reliably available.

The two-part approach to support requests during burnout reduces the cognitive load of the asking. The first part is: I am not managing well at the moment and I need support. This part does not require the parent to know what they need. It communicates that the need exists. The second part is: the most useful thing right now would be one specific practical thing. If you know what the specific thing is, name it. If you do not know, the request can be: the most useful thing right now would be something practical that I do not have to manage or explain.

This two-part structure works because it does not require the neurotypical support person to interpret an implicit need from a non-specific distress communication, which is where most support requests fail. It provides explicit permission to offer specific practical help rather than emotional advice. And it does not require the depleted parent to have performed an accurate internal needs assessment before asking.

Building a Network That Understands the Household

The medium-term support goal is a network in which at least one person in each of the following categories has an accurate working understanding of the household: the practical operational support person, the emotional witness support person, and the professional support person. These three roles may be filled by three different people or, in some cases, by two people across the three functions. The minimum viable support network requires all three functions to be covered.

Building this network is itself a demand, and it is a demand that has to be approached with the same architecture principles from Chapter 7.0: it is built incrementally, with low initiation cost at each step, and it is built during less acute periods rather than attempted during crisis.

Here is how one parent identified and built around her actual support network.

Consider Ivor (name changed), a mother in her late thirties with AuDHD who had been parenting her PDA-profile son for seven years. Ivor had invested heavily in the support structures she had been told were most helpful: regular therapy with a practitioner who specialised in anxiety, attendance at a local parent support group for parents of complex needs children, and close contact with her sister, who was the person in her family most invested in her wellbeing. After eighteen months of consistent engagement with all three, she assessed each honestly. The therapy was providing a space but the framework was wrong: the therapist was skilled but did not understand PDA and consistently generated homework that Ivor could not complete, which produced shame rather than support. The local support group was providing contact with other parents but the experiences were different enough that the witness was incomplete and the advice was sometimes actively wrong for her household. Her sister was the person she felt most loved by and least actually supported by, because the sister's emotional response to Ivor's situation required significant management and produced advice that assumed a different household.

What Ivor found when she looked honestly was that her most consistent source of useful support was a specific online community of AuDHD parents of PDA children, which she had been using for two years but had not classified as real support because it did not match the forms she had been told support should take. The community provided accurate witness, practical wisdom, and the specific absence of the mismatch that characterised every other support interaction. She restructured her support investment: continued the therapy but changed practitioner to one with explicit AuDHD and PDA knowledge, reduced the local group to occasional attendance rather than weekly, had an honest conversation with her sister about what kind of contact was useful and what kind was not, and explicitly elevated the online community to the status of primary support alongside the new therapy. The restructuring reduced her total support contact time but increased the quality and relevance of the support she received. Six months later, she described the change as the most significant structural improvement in her support system she had made in seven years of parenting the household she was actually in.

What This Chapter Has Named

The support gap for the AuDHD parent of a PDA child is real. It is produced by a consistent mismatch between the frameworks from which support is offered and the actual conditions of the household. Neurotypical support frequently generates advice that cannot be implemented in the actual household, producing the secondary cost of the parent managing the mismatch.

Useful support in this context is specific, practical, recurring, and does not require the parent to initiate each instance. It is witness without advice. It is understanding without explanation required.

The support audit identifies what is actually helping versus what carries the social weight of support without providing the function. The minimum viable support network covers three functions: practical operational support, emotional witness, and professional support with framework compatibility. The network is built incrementally, during less acute periods, and around what actually exists rather than what should exist.

The isolation of this experience is real. The communities in which it is shared and understood also exist. Finding them is not a supplementary task. For many AuDHD parents in burnout, it is the most significant support step available.

Chapter 9.0 When Your Child Is Also in Crisis

The Simultaneous Crisis Problem

The burnout literature, what little of it addresses parents at all, tends to treat the recovery problem as if the person can step away from their life while they recover. Take time off. Reduce responsibilities. Create space. What none of it addresses is the parent whose responsibilities include a child who is also in crisis, whose need does not pause, and whose nervous system is actively generating the demand load that is making the parent worse.

For the AuDHD parent of a PDA child, the simultaneous crisis is not unusual. It is the expected condition in the late stages of unaddressed burnout. The parenting relationship has been under increasing strain for months. The child, who is acutely sensitive to the parent's internal state, has been registering the parent's depletion as a relational threat and responding with escalated anxiety and demand avoidance. The parent's reduced capacity has made the low-demand environment harder to sustain, which has increased the child's threat activation. By the time the parent's burnout is acute, the child is frequently in a sustained crisis of their own: school refusal, extended shutdown periods, significant behavioral escalation, or complete withdrawal.

The simultaneous crisis problem does not have a clean solution. This chapter does not offer one. It offers something more specific: a way to survive the simultaneous crisis without the mutual dysregulation cycle destroying the relationship that, when everything else has reduced to its minimum, is the single most protective factor for the PDA child.

Why Your Burnout Affects Your Child's Regulation

The parent's internal state is the primary regulatory environment for the child, regardless of how old the child is and regardless of how much the parent believes they are successfully concealing their internal state. Daniel Siegel and Mary Hartzell's work on parental state and co-regulation has documented that children read the parent's nervous system state through a range of channels, including tone of voice, facial expression, movement quality, and the micro-signals of arousal that the parent may not be consciously producing but that the child's nervous system is continuously scanning for (Siegel and Hartzell, 2003).

For the PDA child, whose nervous system is already calibrated to a higher level of ambient threat-detection than a neurotypical child's, this regulatory reading is even more significant. The PDA profile involves a nervous system that is continuously assessing the safety level of the environment, including the safety level of the relational environment. The parent in burnout is carrying a high autonomic activation level that the child's threat-detection system registers as a signal that the environment is unsafe, even when the parent is not behaving in obviously distressed ways, even when the parent is making every effort to present as calm.

The child's behavioral response to this registered threat is not defiance and not a deliberate expression of the parent's burnout. It is the automatic output of a PDA nervous system in threat-detection mode: more demand avoidance, more dysregulation, more need for co-regulation from the parent who has the least available to give. The child is not making the burnout worse on purpose. They are responding to the burnout with the only nervous system they have.

Why Your Child's Crisis Deepens Your Burnout

The amplification works in both directions, and this is the feature of the simultaneous crisis that receives no attention in standard burnout or parenting support literature.

The parent's burnout impairs the specific capacities most required by PDA parenting. The flexible, indirect communication that reduces the PDA child's threat activation requires the executive function that ADHD depletion has specifically removed. The emotional regulation that allows the parent to remain a calm co-regulatory presence requires the parasympathetic nervous system access that autistic burnout has specifically impaired. The repair conversations that follow difficult moments require the cognitive and emotional resources that are most depleted in the triple-layer burnout state.

Each of the PDA child's dysregulated episodes during the parent's burnout costs more to the parent than the same episode would cost in a less depleted state. The cost per incident is higher. The recovery time between incidents is longer. The accumulation of high-cost interactions over days and weeks is itself a depletion mechanism, not just a symptom of depletion. And the parent who is aware, even partially, of the degree to which their own burnout is contributing to the child's crisis is carrying the additional weight of guilt and self-criticism that is itself a physiological cost on the already depleted system.

Raymaker and colleagues documented that the parenting capacity of autistic adults in burnout was specifically and significantly impaired, and that participants reported the awareness of their own reduced parenting capacity as among the most distressing features of the burnout experience (Raymaker et al., 2020). The distress about the parenting is not separate from the burnout. It is part of it.

The Mutual Dysregulation Cycle

The mutual dysregulation cycle has a structure that becomes visible when it is mapped. The parent's burnout increases the ambient threat signal in the household. The PDA child's nervous system registers the increased threat signal and responds with escalated demand avoidance and dysregulation. The escalated child behavior increases the parent's demand load at the moment of lowest capacity. The increased demand load deepens the parent's burnout. The deepened burnout increases the ambient threat signal further. The cycle accelerates.

The cycle does not require either party to be doing anything wrong. Both the parent's burnout response and the child's PDA response are neurologically appropriate responses to the conditions they are in. The parent is depleted and cannot sustain the resources required by the high-demand environment. The child's nervous system is registering genuine threat signals and responding with genuine threat-responses. The problem is not one of failure. It is one of two nervous systems, each doing what their neurology dictates, in a combination that amplifies both.

The cycle's escalation is not infinite. It reaches breaking points of different kinds: school refusal, medical crisis, family breakdown, or the parent simply stopping, not through choice but through complete functional collapse. The work of this chapter is to introduce a different intervention point before the cycle reaches those breaking points.

Ross and Sparrow's research on PDA and family stress documented the specific escalation patterns in PDA households during periods of parental stress, finding that the relationship between parental wellbeing and child behavioral presentation was more tightly coupled in PDA families than in comparison families, and that interventions focused on parental regulatory capacity produced more significant effects on child behavior than interventions targeted at the child's behavior directly (Ross and Sparrow, 2019). This finding has a direct implication for the simultaneous crisis: what helps the parent most also helps the child most, because the parent's regulatory state is the most significant environmental variable for the PDA child's nervous system.

Triage When Both of You Are in Crisis

When the mutual dysregulation cycle is at its worst, the parent cannot do everything they would normally try to do. The attempt to do everything is itself a demand that the depleted system will fail to meet, and the failure produces additional depletion through the self-critical response that follows. The triage in this situation is stark: identify the one thing that absolutely must stay intact, reduce everything else to its minimum, and accept that minimum as sufficient for this period.

The triage framework for simultaneous crisis has three levels. The first level is safety: the child is not in physical danger, the parent is not in a state that poses risk to the child or to themselves. This level is non-negotiable and must be assessed and addressed before any other consideration. The second level is the relationship anchor: the one daily interaction or connection point that keeps the parent-child relationship alive and present even when the practical parenting has reduced to its minimum. The third level is the functional minimum: the specific subset of the Chapter 5.0 minimum viable household that can be sustained in the simultaneous crisis period.

Everything outside those three levels is, for the duration of the crisis period, accepted as currently beyond capacity. Not failed. Not abandoned. Accepted as currently unavailable, in the same way that a person in a medical crisis accepts that they cannot currently perform at their usual professional level. The standards applied to the simultaneous crisis period are the standards appropriate to the crisis, not the standards appropriate to the recovered state.

The One Thing That Has to Stay Intact

In the simultaneous crisis, when everything is reduced and failing and the parent cannot sustain the parenting approach they know the PDA child needs, there is one thing that has to stay as intact as possible: the child's felt sense that the parent is still there for them. Not performing well. Not managing. Not sustaining the low-demand household at the standard it requires. There for them.

The parent who has reduced to their minimum, who is surviving rather than thriving, who cannot maintain the communication indirectness or the co-regulation or the repair conversations at the standard they would in a better state, can still produce one signal that the child's nervous system can register as safety: I am still here. I am not going anywhere. This difficulty is not you losing me.

That signal does not require the parent to be recovered. It does not require the parent to have resources they do not have. It requires the smallest possible reliable presence: a consistent daily moment, however brief, of genuine contact, without demands in either direction, that tells the child's nervous system that the relational environment is not collapsing even if the functional environment is.

Siegel and Hartzell's work on the repair of ruptures in the parent-child relationship documents that children are more resilient to parental difficulty than parents typically believe, provided the relationship itself remains navigable and repair is present (Siegel and Hartzell, 2003). The child who knows that the parent's difficult period is a difficult period, and not a permanent withdrawal, has a different neurological experience of that difficulty than the child who experiences it as abandonment. The parent in simultaneous crisis does not need to protect the child from the difficulty. They need to protect the child's understanding that the relationship survives it.

What Good Enough Parenting Looks Like During Burnout

Good enough parenting during burnout does not look like good parenting. It does not look like the PDA-informed, flexible, low-demand, co-regulatory parenting that the parent has been learning to provide. It looks like staying in the room when it is very hard to stay in the room. It looks like not saying the thing that would make the situation worse when the depleted system is generating the impulse to say it. It looks like a ten-minute shared activity with no demands when thirty minutes of therapeutic co-regulation is not available. It looks like I know this is hard right now, said in a quiet voice when nothing else is possible.

Kristin Neff's work on self-compassion is directly applicable here, specifically the principle that self-compassion in difficult moments is not the lowering of standards but the application of the same compassion to oneself that one would offer a person one cares about in the same circumstances (Neff, 2011). The parent who is asking whether they are a good enough parent during the burnout crisis would, if asked about a close friend in the same situation, not apply the standards of recovered, full-capacity, optimally-informed PDA parenting. They would apply the standards of: are they still there? Are they trying? Is the child safe? Is the relationship surviving?

Applied to themselves, those same compassionate standards produce a more accurate assessment of what is actually required, and release the self-critical load that the gap between full-capacity standards and burnout-capacity performance has been generating. That release is itself a small but real resource recovery.

Protecting the Relationship When You Cannot Protect Anything Else

The relationship with the PDA child is the most important thing the parent is protecting in the simultaneous crisis period, because it is the most protective factor for the child's long-term wellbeing and because it is the foundation on which the parenting, when the parent recovers capacity, will rebuild.

Protecting the relationship in a burnout period does not look like maintaining the relationship's normal quality. It looks like keeping the relationship present and survivable. The specific actions that keep the relationship present and survivable during the simultaneous crisis are small, low-demand, and consistent. They do not require the parent to be recovered. They require the parent to be reliably present at the anchor point.

The anchor point is whatever daily contact has the lowest demand threshold in both directions. It is not the therapeutic conversation, the careful repair dialogue, the co-regulation session. It is the thing that the parent and child can do together that costs almost nothing and asks almost nothing of either nervous system. Sitting together watching a preferred screen. A brief shared activity around a special interest. A short physical proximity without conversation. The value of the anchor point is its consistency, not its quality. The child who can predict that the anchor point will be there, every day, regardless of what the rest of the day contained, has a nervous system anchor in the relational environment that the burnout period cannot remove.

The Repair That Does Not Require Full Recovery First

One of the most persistent barriers to the parent taking care of the relationship during the simultaneous crisis is the sense that repair requires resources the parent does not currently have. The idea that before things can be repaired, the parent has to be recovered enough to do the repair properly. This frame keeps the repair from happening during the period when both systems are in crisis, and it misunderstands what repair actually requires in this context.

Repair in the PDA parenting context, during burnout, does not look like the thorough, emotionally attuned, carefully paced repair conversation that the parent would produce in a better state. It looks like: I know the last few weeks have been hard for both of us. I am not managing well at the moment and that has affected what I can give you. That is not your fault and it is not forever.

That statement, in whatever words the parent can find, does not require full recovery. It requires enough honesty to name the reality that the child has already registered, enough warmth to communicate that the naming comes from care rather than withdrawal, and enough consistency to repeat it at intervals during the hard period. The child whose parent names the difficulty, even imperfectly, has a different neurological relationship to that difficulty than the child for whom it remains unnamed and therefore potentially threatening.

The repair that does not require full recovery first is the repair available now, in the burnout. It is not the optimal repair. It is the repair that keeps the relationship survivable. And keeping the relationship survivable is, in the simultaneous crisis, the whole of what the parenting has to achieve.

Here is how one parent managed this.

Consider Jory (name changed), a parent in their early thirties with AuDHD whose nine-year-old daughter had a PDA profile. During a period of acute burnout that coincided with their daughter's school refusal escalating to complete non-attendance, Jory was attempting to maintain the full low-demand parenting approach while also managing the school communication, the professional support appointments, the home education provision, and their own reduced professional workload. All of it was failing. The daughter's anxiety was escalating in direct proportion to the pressure Jory was placing on themselves to provide the full therapeutic parenting environment. Everything Jory attempted as a recovery step was consumed by the continuing demands before it could restore anything.

The shift came when Jory stopped trying to maintain the full environment and identified the single anchor that could survive the crisis. Their daughter had a shared interest in a particular animated series. Every day, regardless of how the rest of the day had gone, regardless of what had escalated or refused or shut down, they sat together for ten minutes and watched one episode.

No discussion of what was happening. No therapeutic framing. No demands from either direction. The daughter chose the episode. They watched it together. That was the whole of it. The anchor point cost Jory almost nothing in resource terms. It was not a performance of parenting. It was a genuine ten minutes of shared presence. Over six weeks, the daughter's baseline anxiety level reduced. Not because anything else had changed. Because the anchor point told her nervous system, every single day, that the relational environment was still safe even while everything else was hard.

What This Chapter Has Named

The simultaneous crisis of AuDHD parent burnout and PDA child escalation is the expected outcome of the mutual dysregulation cycle, not a sign of particular failure. The cycle has a neurological structure: the parent's burnout increases the ambient threat signal, the child's PDA nervous system escalates in response, the escalation deepens the parent's burnout, and the depletion deepens the child's crisis.

The chapter does not offer a way out of the cycle. It offers a way to prevent the cycle from destroying the relationship that is the most protective factor for the PDA child. The triage is clear: safety first, relationship anchor second, functional minimum third, everything else accepted as currently beyond capacity.

Good enough parenting during burnout is staying present, not making things worse, and finding the one daily anchor that tells the child's nervous system the relationship is still there. The repair that does not require full recovery first is the naming of the difficulty, simply and honestly, so the child does not have to carry it alone.

The relationship survives the burnout if the parent lets it be enough, for now, that it survives.

Chapter 10.0 The Sustainable Floor

From Recovery to Sustainability

The work of the preceding chapters has been about the acute phase: recognising the burnout, reducing the demand load, building recovery windows, identifying support, surviving the periods when both parent and child are in crisis. That work is necessary, and it is the foundation on which everything else depends. But it is not the final destination. The final destination is a life that does not periodically cycle back into the acute phase, that does not require the same crash-and-recover pattern that has characterised the previous years, that is sustainable across the full complexity of the actual household, in the actual person's actual nervous system.

This chapter addresses the transition from recovery to sustainability. Not from crisis to optimal function. From crisis to a stable operating floor that can be maintained without periodic collapse. The sustainable floor is not a comfortable place by the standards of what most people imagine their life should be. It is lower than that. It is the realistic assessment of what this parent, with this neurology, in this household, can maintain consistently without depletion accelerating. And it is more stable and more useful than the high-function bursts followed by collapse cycles that characterise unaddressed AuDHD burnout in the PDA parenting context.

Why Recovery Without Architecture Leads Back to Burnout

Most AuDHD parents who recover from a burnout episode return to the same structural conditions that produced the burnout, and they return to them faster than they expect, because the recovery itself tends to free up resource that the pre-burnout pattern immediately reclaims. The parent who recovers three hours of weekly capacity quickly discovers that three hours of outstanding obligations, relationships, and commitments have been waiting to reclaim exactly that much space. The recovery does not produce a new stable state. It restores capacity to a structure that was already operating beyond sustainable limits before the burnout, and the cycle begins again.

Barkley's work on ADHD and lifestyle design has documented this pattern in ADHD adults more broadly, finding that the executive function deficits that produce the original overcommitment also prevent the self-monitoring that would detect early warning signs of the next collapse, and that without deliberate structural change in the external environment, the pattern tends to repeat at consistent intervals (Barkley, 2012). For the AuDHD parent, those consistent intervals are visible in retrospect, once the pattern is identified. The Burnout has probably happened before. In some cases it has happened multiple times, recognised or not, at intervals of months to a few years.

Recovery without architecture is recovery into the same conditions. The architecture is what changes the conditions so that the recovered capacity is not immediately reclaimed by the structure that consumed it in the first place.

The Structural Factors That Caused This Burnout

Before building the sustainable floor, the structural factors that produced this burnout need to be identified. Not the immediate triggers, which are usually visible and often already addressed through the Chapter 5.0 audit. The underlying structural conditions that made the immediate triggers intolerable rather than manageable.

The structural factor audit looks at five categories. The first is the demand ceiling: what is the maximum sustainable demand load for this parent's neurology in this household, and how far above that ceiling was the pre-burnout operating level? The gap between the ceiling and the pre-burnout level is the structural problem. The immediate triggers are events that pushed the already-above-ceiling system into collapse.

The second category is the support deficit: what support was absent that would have prevented the burnout if it had been present? Not the support that appeared after the burnout. The support that, had it been in place before, would have kept the demand load within the ceiling.

The third category is the accommodation gap: what accommodations for the AuDHD profile were not in place, at work, in relationships, or in the household, that would have reduced the cost per unit of demand?

The fourth category is the recovery deficit: what recovery was absent from the structure, not as an add-on but as a built-in component of the daily and weekly pattern?

The fifth category is the warning signal failure: what physical and functional signals appeared in the months before the burnout that were not registered or acted on? The Chapter 2.0 and Chapter 4.0 work is relevant here. Most burnouts, when mapped retrospectively, show clear escalating warning signals for three to six months before the collapse. The signals were present. The systems for registering and acting on them were not.

Identifying Your Personal Burnout Accelerators

Within the structural factors are specific accelerators: the conditions, events, or patterns that most reliably and most quickly move the parent's system from manageable depletion toward burnout. Identifying the individual accelerators allows the sustainable floor to be built with specific protections around those high-risk areas rather than attempting to reduce demand across the board, which is less efficient and less targeted.

Common burnout accelerators in the AuDHD parent population include: sustained social performance demands such as school meetings, professional contexts, or extended family gatherings; periods of household routine disruption such as school holidays, illness, or significant life events; cumulative sleep disruption beyond a threshold the parent's specific system can tolerate; increased masking demands from any source; and periods of the child's elevated crisis that extend beyond the parent's co-regulation reserve.

The personal accelerator mapping uses the same external tracking approach described in Chapter 4.0. The parent maps the previous burnout episode, and any previous episodes they can identify, looking for the conditions that appeared in the weeks before collapse. The conditions that appear consistently across multiple episodes are the personal accelerators. The conditions that appeared once or in unusual circumstances are less predictive. The consistent ones are the targets for the sustainable floor's specific protective structures.

Yehuda and Lehrner's research on intergenerational stress has documented how chronic stress responses can produce lasting alterations in the stress threshold, such that subsequent stress events produce faster and more acute responses than the same events would have produced before the initial chronic stress (Yehuda and Lehrner, 2018). The implication for the AuDHD parent who has been through multiple burnout cycles is that the threshold for the next cycle may be lower than the threshold for the first. The sustainable floor's protective structures need to be calibrated to the current threshold, not the threshold that existed before the burnout pattern was established.

The Sustainable Floor: What It Is and How to Find Yours

The sustainable floor is the operating level at which the parent can function consistently, month over month, without the depletion rate exceeding the recovery rate. It is characterised by the absence of net depletion rather than by the presence of optimal functioning. The parent on their sustainable floor is not thriving in the conventional sense. They are maintaining.

Consistently, reliably, without the periodic collapse that characterises the burnout cycle.

Finding the sustainable floor requires honest calibration at three levels. The first is the demand ceiling: what is the maximum weekly demand load the parent can sustain without net depletion? This is lower than the pre-burnout operating level. For many AuDHD parents, it is significantly lower. The honest calibration does not flinch from this reality.

The second level is the recovery floor: what is the minimum weekly recovery that keeps the depletion rate at or below the recovery rate? This is the quantity of recovery that has to be built into the structure before any other consideration, because it is the mechanism that prevents net depletion from accumulating.

The third level is the buffer zone: what is the quantity of reserve capacity that needs to be maintained above the operating level to absorb the inevitable spikes in demand that the PDA household produces without driving the system above the depletion ceiling? The sustainable floor includes a buffer. The parent who operates at exactly their ceiling has no capacity to absorb the dysregulation episode, the school communication, the medical appointment, the unexpected financial event. The buffer is the difference between a sustainable floor and a floor that collapses every time something unexpected happens.

Raymaker and colleagues' research on burnout prevention in autistic adults identified that the most significant predictor of not re-entering burnout following recovery was the presence of structural changes in the operating environment that reduced the sustained demand load below the individual's identified threshold (Raymaker et al., 2020). The structural changes are not achieved through better self-management. They are achieved through changes in the external conditions: the obligations removed, the accommodations put in place, the support built in, the standards reduced to what the floor can actually sustain.

Building a Household That Does Not Require Maximum Effort

The household that produced the burnout was a household that required near-maximum effort to sustain. Not because the parent was doing something wrong. Because the household was configured, through accumulated obligation, maintained standard, and absent support, at a level that required more than the parent's sustained capacity. The burnout was the proof.

Building a household that does not require maximum effort requires the same categories of structural change that the Chapter 5.0 audit identified, but as permanent structural features rather than emergency measures. The good enough threshold that was introduced as a crisis response becomes the permanent standard. The delegated and automated functions that were introduced to survive the burnout become the permanent infrastructure. The obligations that were deferred become obligations that are permanently removed rather than reinstated when capacity returns.

This is the part of the sustainable floor work that most AuDHD parents find hardest. Not because the changes are difficult to make, but because the internal rule system and the identity investment in managing well resist the permanence of the reduction. The parent who reduced their household standards during the burnout as a crisis measure can tolerate it as temporary. The parent who accepts that the reduced standard is the appropriate standard for their household and neurology, permanently, is making a different kind of claim. A claim about what their life actually requires rather than what they believed it should require.

Siegel's work on neuroplasticity and sustainable change has documented that lasting change in function and wellbeing is associated with changes in the structural environment rather than with changes in self-regulation effort, and that the self-regulation effort required to maintain a change decreases as the structural environment adapts to support the new pattern (Siegel, 2012). The sustainable floor is most reliably maintained when it is supported by the external architecture and least reliably maintained when it depends on the ongoing internal effort of the person trying to sustain it.

Pacing Across the Week, Month, and Year

The sustainable floor has a temporal dimension that operates at three scales: weekly, monthly, and annual.

Weekly pacing applies the sustainable floor logic to the structure of each week. The total demand load in any given week should not exceed the ceiling by more than the buffer allows. High-demand days are balanced by low-demand days. The meso-recovery sessions from Chapter 7.0 are the primary weekly pacing mechanism. The weekly structure is reviewed regularly and adjusted when the accumulated demand in a given week would breach the ceiling without buffer to absorb it.

Monthly pacing recognises that some months are structurally higher-demand than others, regardless of the choices made within them. The school calendar creates predictable high-demand periods: term start, parent evenings, report cycles, transition points. The family calendar creates predictable high-demand periods: birthdays, school holidays, medical review cycles, financial events. Monthly pacing maps these predictable high-demand periods in advance and applies proactive demand reduction in the two to three weeks before each identified high-demand period. Not waiting until the high-demand period has produced depletion, but reducing the load before it arrives so the buffer is intact when it does.

Annual pacing extends the monthly pacing logic to the full year. The parent who can identify their historically highest burnout-risk quarters can apply proactive structural demand reduction in those quarters as a permanent feature of the annual architecture. The reductions are not emergency measures. They are the planned operating level for that quarter, built into the annual structure in advance, so that the high-risk period is met with a system that has been operating below its ceiling rather than at or above it.

Early Warning Systems for the Next Burnout Cycle

The sustainable floor includes an early warning system: a set of specific, pre-identified signals that indicate the floor is being breached and the system is beginning to move toward the next burnout cycle. The signals are the same physical and functional markers identified in Chapters 2.0 and 4.0. The early warning system is the structured process for monitoring them and triggering a response before the breach becomes a cascade.

The monitoring process needs to be as low-demand as the daily tracking described in Chapter 4.0, because the early warning system will be used most when the system is already under the most pressure. The weekly signal review is the minimum: a five-minute check against the personal early warning indicators list, identifying whether any signals are present and whether the pattern is consistent with the pre-burnout escalation profile identified in the structural factors audit.

The response protocol is pre-decided and written into the blueprint from Chapter 7.0. When signal cluster one appears, the response is the specific demand reduction or recovery increase already identified. When signal cluster two appears, the response escalates to the next tier. The response does not require the depleted system to generate a plan in real time. The plan exists. The signal triggers the plan.

What Sustainable Looks Like in Practice

The sustainable floor is not a dramatic transformation. It does not look like thriving by most definitions. It looks like a household that functions consistently at a lower standard than the pre-burnout household, with a parent who is less productive, less socially active, and less visibly impressive than the pre-burnout version, and who is not periodically collapsing into a state of complete functional failure. It looks, from the outside, like someone who has set their expectations lower than they should. From the inside, it is the most functional state the system can reliably sustain.

Consider Kenrick (name changed), a father in his mid-forties with AuDHD who had been parenting his PDA-profile son for eleven years. Kenrick had experienced what he retrospectively identified as four or five significant burnout episodes across those eleven years, none of which he had understood as burnout at the time. When he mapped his previous eighteen months in detail, using the physical signal tracking and the demand load data he had been collecting as part of his recovery work, a pattern became visible that he had never seen before. The burnout was cycling on an approximately four-month schedule. The high-demand periods were consistently the same: the autumn school term start in September, the extended family Christmas period in December, the spring school review period in March, and the summer transition period in July. His recovery periods, such as they were, occupied the quieter intervals between those peaks. He had been managing the crisis, not the pattern.

Using the annual pacing approach, Kenrick identified the four annually occurring high-demand periods and built a quarterly demand reduction strategy around them. In the six weeks before each identified high-demand quarter, he applied a specific set of demand reductions: reduced professional commitments, suspended the social obligations that he knew from his support audit were consuming more than they were providing, and activated the macro-recovery arrangements from his Chapter 7.0 blueprint. The demand reduction was modest. He was not withdrawing from functioning. He was arriving at the high-demand period with buffer intact rather than already depleted. The following year, for the first time in eleven years of parenting the household, he did not enter an acute burnout episode at any of the four historically high-risk points. Not because his life was easier. Because he had mapped the cycle and designed around it before it consumed him again.

What This Chapter Has Named

The sustainable floor is the long-term destination of the recovery work: not optimal function, but consistent, non-collapsing function across the full complexity of the AuDHD parent's actual household and neurology. It is lower than most people want it to be. It is more stable and more useful than the burnout cycle.

Building the sustainable floor requires honest calibration of the demand ceiling, the recovery floor, and the buffer zone. It requires structural changes in the household that are permanent rather than crisis-period, including the maintained good enough threshold, the built-in recovery architecture, and the proactive demand reductions around historically high-risk periods.

Pacing across the week, month, and year translates the sustainable floor into a temporal structure that anticipates rather than reacts. The early warning system ensures that the next burnout cycle, if it begins, is intercepted before it becomes a cascade.

The sustainable floor is not the life the AuDHD parent imagined they would have. It is the life their actual nervous system can support, in their actual household, with the actual PDA parenting complexity they are navigating. That life, consistently maintained, is more available to the parent, and more protective for the child, than the life they have been trying to sustain at the cost of periodic collapse.

Chapter 11.0 You Were Not Built Wrong

What the Burnout Was Actually Saying

There is a story most AuDHD parents tell themselves about their burnout. The story goes: I should have been able to manage this. Other people manage households more complex than mine without collapsing. I have had the same struggles my whole life, which means the problem is something fundamental about me. The burnout is the proof. The burnout is my limit. The burnout is the point at which my inadequacy became impossible to hide.

Every part of that story is wrong. Not wrong in the sense that it can be replaced by a more positive story. Wrong in the factual sense. Wrong in the direction it locates the cause. The burnout is not evidence that the parent was inadequate to the conditions. The burnout is evidence that the conditions were inadequate to the parent.

The burnout was saying: the demand load has exceeded the recovery capacity for a sustained period. The burnout was saying: the nervous system is operating without the accommodation structures it requires to function sustainably. The burnout was saying: the co-regulation demands of PDA parenting, the masking demands of neurotypical environments, the executive demands of a depleted ADHD system operating without external scaffolding, have collectively exceeded what any nervous system in this configuration can sustain without adequate support. The burnout was not saying anything about the parent's worth, capability, or fundamental adequacy. It was reporting the outcome of a structural mismatch between what the nervous system requires and what the environment provided.

That is a different message entirely. This chapter is about receiving it accurately.

The Conditions That Produced It Were Real

The AuDHD parent in triple-layer burnout has almost invariably been told, at some point in the burnout, that the conditions they are describing are manageable. That other families have similarly complex situations and manage without crisis. That the right strategies, the right support, the right attitude, the right approach would produce a different outcome. The implicit message is that the conditions are not the problem. The person's response to the conditions is the problem.

This is the specific inversion that Raymaker and colleagues documented as one of the most consistent features of the autistic burnout experience: the systematic attribution of burnout to personal inadequacy rather than to the structural mismatch between the person's neurodevelopmental profile and the environment's demands (Raymaker et al., 2020). It is not a misunderstanding individual people make about individual AuDHD parents. It is a systematic cultural pattern, produced by a framework that locates the cause of difficulty inside the person rather than in the relationship between the person and their conditions.

The conditions that produced this burnout were real. The AuDHD parent was running three simultaneous depletion processes: the autistic burnout produced by sustained masking, sensory overload, and the absence of accommodation; the ADHD depletion produced by executive demands without scaffolding; and the PDA parenting exhaustion produced by a household that generates the specific type of relational demand most costly to the autistic nervous system. Any one of those depletion processes would be significant in isolation. Together, interacting with and amplifying each other, they were producing a demand load that the clinical literature specifically identifies as unsustainable without structural support. The support was not there. The burnout was the outcome. The outcome was correct.

The Reframe That Is Actually True

The reframe this chapter offers is not the positive reframe. It is not: you are actually doing brilliantly, this is so hard, look how well you are managing. That reframe is kind in intention and false in content, and false content does not produce the neurological state that sustainable recovery requires.

The reframe that is actually true is: the burnout was the accurate physiological response of a nervous system that was asked to operate beyond its sustainable capacity without the structural support that would have made it sustainable. That nervous system is not damaged. It is functional. It reported accurately. The problem the burnout identified is a structural problem, and structural problems have structural solutions.

Schmitt and colleagues' work on justice sensitivity is relevant here: individuals with high justice sensitivity, which is well represented in the autistic and ADHD populations, respond with particular intensity to situations of perceived inequity, including the specific inequity of being held responsible for outcomes produced by structural failures (Schmitt et al., 1995). The AuDHD parent who has been implicitly held responsible for the outcome of a structural mismatch, who has internalised that responsibility as evidence of inadequacy, is experiencing a justice violation that the burnout's self-blame narrative perpetuates. Naming the structural source of the burnout is not just an intellectual reframe. It is a correction of an injustice that the parent has been carrying, often for years.

The true reframe is: you were not built wrong. The support architecture you needed was not built. These are different problems. Only one of them is about you.

What You Have Built Despite the Conditions

The clinical picture of triple-layer burnout emphasises what has been lost or impaired. The executive function that is not working.

The sensory tolerance that has collapsed. The emotional capacity that has been depleted. The recovery capacity that is insufficient. This emphasis is accurate and necessary for the assessment and intervention work this book has described. It is also incomplete.

The AuDHD parent in triple-layer burnout has, in the same period that produced the burnout, been maintaining a household, a parenting relationship, and some version of a professional and social presence. They have been doing this in conditions that would produce significant impairment in any nervous system without the specific resilience features of the AuDHD profile. They have been doing it without the structural support that clinical frameworks identify as necessary. They have been doing it while simultaneously experiencing the unrecognised grief of late diagnosis, the identity disruption of burnout, and the specific relational stress of PDA parenting in a world that does not understand PDA.

Hermelin's research on capability under adversity documented how individuals operating under chronic high-demand conditions without adequate support consistently underestimate their own functional level, because their reference point for normal performance is the high-demand condition rather than the baseline their nervous system would achieve with appropriate support (Hermelin, 2001). The AuDHD parent in burnout is not seeing what they have managed against the backdrop of the conditions they were managing in. They are seeing only the gap between what they managed and what they believe they should have managed without those conditions. The gap looks like failure. It is not.

The Specific Strengths That Burnout Cannot Take

The burnout depletes specific systems. It does not deplete everything. The features of the AuDHD profile that have been most costly in the conditions this parent has been navigating are not only costs. They are also the source of specific capabilities that the burnout did not produce and cannot take.

The intensity of commitment that made the PDA parenting approach possible in the first place: the sustained dedication to understanding the child's nervous system, the willingness to unlearn what the mainstream parenting culture said and replace it with what the specific child needed, the persistence of the research and the reading and the rethinking. That is not a neurotypical feature. It is a feature of the specific depth of engagement and interest that the AuDHD profile generates when it is focused on something that matters. The burnout did not produce that commitment. It could not remove it.

The directness that makes the communication hard in some contexts is the same feature that makes it trustworthy in the contexts where honesty is what is needed. The precision that makes transitioning exhausting is the same feature that produces the specific competence in the areas of genuine interest. The sensory processing that makes certain environments unbearable is the same feature that produces the specific richness of perceptual experience that the AuDHD adult has access to when the environment is calibrated. The pattern recognition that makes certain kinds of cognitive work effortless is the same feature that allowed the burnout parent to eventually identify the patterns in their child's nervous system that the professionals were missing.

These are not compensations or silver linings. They are features. They are the same features that produced the costs. And they are not burnout damage. They are the profile. The profile is intact at the bottom of the burnout, waiting for the conditions that allow it to function.

What Comes After This Book

This book has not resolved the AuDHD parent's situation. It was not designed to. The PDA child is still in the household. The triple-layer depletion system is still present. The structural conditions that produced the burnout have not been fully addressed by reading a book about them. The parent who finishes this book and expects to find themselves in a different household is going to be disappointed in a specific way that this chapter wants to name before it happens.

What this book has done is provide a framework for understanding what was previously incomprehensible. The cascade that seemed like a personal failing now has a structure, a name, three identified layers, and a research base. The rest that was not working is now understood to be a specific type of rest that was never going to work for this nervous system and not evidence that rest itself was impossible. The support that was not helpful is now understood to be support from a framework that did not fit the actual household. The child's behavior is now understood through a model that does not locate its cause in the parent's inadequacy. The burnout is now understood as a structural outcome of structural conditions.

Understanding is not recovery. But it is the prerequisite for the kind of recovery that does not simply reset the same conditions. Research on late-diagnosed neurodivergent adults has consistently documented how access to an accurate diagnostic framework represents the single most significant turning point in their recovery journey—more transformative than any specific intervention. Corden et al.'s landmark study found that diagnosis led to "a post-diagnostic process that included emotional reactions and self-exploration, which developed into self-acceptance and belonging," fundamentally changing participants' relationship to their past struggles (Corden et al., 2021). Leedham et al.'s research with late-diagnosed autistic women captured this transformation powerfully, with one participant describing: "almost like I was revisiting my whole life and realized, actually I'm not a bad person, I'm not faulty" (Leedham et al., 2020). This reframing process transforms the meaning of lifelong experiences from evidence of personal deficiency to evidence of specific neurological differences navigating structural challenges designed for different brain types (Young et al., 2018). The framework is not the destination. It is the map.

The Household You Are Still Building

The PDA parenting literature consistently identifies the long-term relationship between the PDA child and their primary caregiver as the most significant predictor of the child's eventual outcomes. Not the specific parenting approach that was implemented. Not the professional support that was accessed. Not the school that was found or not found. The relationship. The sustained, repaired, maintained, imperfect, honestly-engaged relationship between the child and the parent who stayed.

The AuDHD parent in burnout has been building and maintaining that relationship under conditions that make it harder than it would otherwise be, with resources that have been reduced by three simultaneous depletion processes, in a culture that has consistently failed to understand, support, or accurately describe what they were doing. The relationship has been fractured and repaired more times than they would have chosen. The parenting has looked worse than they wanted it to on more days than they can count. And the relationship is still there.

That relationship is the household they are still building. Not the physical household, the cleaning standards and the meal planning and the school run logistics. Not the professional household, the career management and the financial structure. The relational household: the specific, ongoing, continuously rebuilt connection between this parent and this child. It is the most important thing they are building. It is the thing the burnout was most threatening. And it is the thing that, on the evidence of this parent's sustained presence in the middle of the conditions this book has described, they have continued to build.

You Were Not Built Wrong. The Support Was.

The parent who comes to this final chapter after reading the preceding ten has been through the assessment of what is depleted and how, the audit of what can be reduced and what must be protected, the architecture of what recovery actually requires for this specific nervous system, the support structures that actually help and those that consistently do not, the identity question that the burnout forces open, and the sustainable floor that prevents the same collapse from recurring. That is not nothing. That is, in fact, the structural support that should have been available from the beginning.

The support that was not built was not just the specific recovery architecture this book describes. It was the diagnostic framework that would have identified the AuDHD profile before the masking strategies became identity. It was the professional understanding of PDA that would have reframed the parenting challenge as a neurological one rather than a behavioral one from the beginning. It was the cultural acknowledgement that the specific intersection of AuDHD parenting and PDA parenting is a real and identifiable configuration that requires specific support structures, not better management. It was the simple, repeated validation that what this parent was experiencing was genuinely as complex as it felt, that the difficulty was in the conditions rather than in the person.

None of that support exists yet at the scale at which it is needed. It is being built, by the researchers this book has cited, by the peer communities in which AuDHD parents of PDA children are finding each other, by the practitioners who are beginning to understand the intersection, and by the parents themselves who are developing frameworks and sharing them with each other because the professional frameworks were not there when they needed them.

You are part of that building. The fact that you are still here, still in the household, still in the relationship, still looking for the understanding that makes the next part survivable: that is not the minimum. That is, under these conditions, a great deal.

You were not built wrong. The support was.

Appendix A Triple-Layer Burnout Self-Assessment Tool

Instructions

This tool is designed for monthly repeat use. It takes under two minutes to complete. Answer each item honestly based on your experience over the past two weeks, not your experience on your best or worst days. Circle or mark the number that most accurately reflects your current state. Do not aim for consistency with previous completions. Each month's result stands alone.

Scoring: 0 = not present / not a problem. 1 = occasionally present, manageable. 2 = frequently present, noticeable impact on function. 3 = consistently present, significant impact on function.

Section 1: Autistic Burnout Indicators

Sensory processing: everyday sounds, lights, or textures that I can usually manage are now regularly exceeding my tolerance level. 0 / 1 / 2 / 3

Masking cost: maintaining my usual social presentation is taking noticeably more effort than it normally does. 0 / 1 / 2 / 3

Shutdown and withdrawal: I am spending more time in shutdown or actively avoiding the sensory environment than I usually would. 0 / 1 / 2 / 3

Communication effort: producing clear speech or written communication is requiring more effort than my usual baseline. 0 / 1 / 2 / 3

Routine disruption impact: changes to my usual routine are producing a stronger reaction than they normally would. 0 / 1 / 2 / 3

Section 1 Total: ___ / 15

Section 2: ADHD Depletion Indicators

Task initiation: I am finding it difficult to start tasks that I know how to do and want to do. 0 / 1 / 2 / 3

Working memory: I am losing track of information mid-task or mid-conversation more frequently than usual. 0 / 1 / 2 / 3

Emotional regulation: my emotional responses are more intense or faster to arrive than my usual baseline. 0 / 1 / 2 / 3

Sustained attention: I am finding it harder than usual to sustain focus on tasks that require concentration. 0 / 1 / 2 / 3

Decision fatigue: making decisions, including small ones, is producing more exhaustion than it usually does. 0 / 1 / 2 / 3

Section 2 Total: ___ / 15

Section 3: PDA Parenting Exhaustion Indicators

Co-regulation demand: the effort of managing my own regulation while also supporting my child's regulation is exceeding my available resource. 0 / 1 / 2 / 3

Indirect communication cost: the sustained effort of maintaining collaborative, low-demand communication is depleting me beyond my usual recovery capacity. 0 / 1 / 2 / 3

Repair capacity: after difficult interactions with my child, I am finding it harder than usual to access the resource for repair. 0 / 1 / 2 / 3

Anticipatory load: I am spending significant energy anticipating and planning around my child's nervous system demands rather than responding to what is actually happening. 0 / 1 / 2 / 3

Relational endurance: the sustained nature of the parenting relationship is feeling heavier than my capacity to carry it in this period. 0 / 1 / 2 / 3

Section 3 Total: ___ / 15

Scoring Guide

Total score 0-9: Functioning within sustainable range. Recovery architecture is maintaining the floor. Continue monitoring monthly.

Total score 10-19: Early depletion signs present across one or more layers. Review the recovery architecture. Identify which layer is highest. Apply targeted micro and meso recovery for that layer. Repeat assessment in two weeks.

Total score 20-29: Significant depletion across multiple layers. The Chapter 5.0 audit is indicated. Review obligation list for immediate reduction. Activate the macro-recovery planning process if a support structure exists. Consult the early warning indicators section of the Recovery Architecture Blueprint.

Total score 30-45: Acute burnout indicators across all three layers. The demand reduction work from Chapter 5.0 is urgent. If macro-recovery support is available, activate it now. If professional support is accessible, this is the point to access it.

Layer Analysis

If one section's score is significantly higher than the others (three or more points above either of the other sections), that layer is the primary acute layer. Apply the specific restoration approach for that layer from Chapter 3.0 before addressing the other layers.

Appendix B The Non-Negotiable Audit Worksheet

Instructions

Complete this audit during a window when you have at least thirty minutes of relative quiet. Do not complete it during an acute crisis period: the executive function and honest self-assessment required are not reliably available during acute depletion. This worksheet is designed to be completed in one sitting but can be returned to across multiple sessions if needed.

Step 1: The Complete Obligation Inventory

List every regular obligation, task, commitment, standard, expectation, and role that you are currently attempting to meet. Include the ones so habitual they barely register as demands. Do not filter. Do not assess. Write.

Use the space below, or a separate page if needed.

[Space for list]

Count your total items: ___

Step 2: The Three Questions

For each item on your list, apply the three questions in order. Move to the next question only if the previous one does not clearly resolve the item's category.

Question 1: If this item did not happen this week, would there be a direct, concrete, irreversible consequence? (Not discomfort, not social disappointment. Irreversible.) If yes: mark as FIXED. If no or uncertain: proceed to Question 2.

Question 2: Is this item on the list because it structurally has to be, or because of history, expectation, guilt, the cost of renegotiation, or agreement made before the current burnout? If primarily history/expectation/guilt: mark as NEGOTIABLE. If genuinely structural but uncertain: proceed to Question 3.

Question 3: If a medical event prevented me from doing this for six months, what would actually happen? If consequences would be manageable or non-existent: mark as DEFERRABLE. If consequences would genuinely be serious: mark as FIXED.

Step 3: Categorisation

Transfer each item to its category column.

FIXED (genuinely non-negotiable, irreversible consequence if removed):

REDUCIBLE (can be done at a lower standard, less frequently, or in a shorter form):

DELEGATABLE (can be done by someone else, even imperfectly):

DEFERRABLE (can pause for a defined period without irreversible consequence):

REMOVABLE (can stop entirely; consequence is only discomfort, guilt, or disappointment):

Step 4: Minimum Viable Household Summary

From your FIXED column only, define the minimum viable household: the specific set of things that actually have to happen for the people in this household to be safe and functional.

Child's essential physical needs that must be met daily:

Parent's essential self-maintenance that must be maintained:

Financial essentials that must be maintained:

Everything else on the FIXED list (record here for reference):

Step 5: Action Plan

From the REMOVABLE category, identify the three items you will act on first:

  1.
  2.
  3.

What communication is needed for each, and when will you send it:

From the DEFERRABLE category, identify the items you will pause and for how long:

From the DELEGATABLE category, identify who can take each item and the specific ask:

Appendix C Recovery Architecture Blueprint

Instructions

This blueprint is a living document. Complete each section as fully as current capacity allows, and return to fill gaps as they become clearer. The completed blueprint should be readable by another adult in a crisis. Write in plain language, not shorthand.

Section 1: Micro-Recovery Map

The micro-recovery map records every identified recovery window in the daily pattern, two to five minutes in length, that is being used as a recovery window rather than a demand window.

For each window, record:

Window 1: Time and trigger (what event starts this window): Duration typically available: Specific activity assigned: What makes this window unavailable on bad days:

Window 2: Time and trigger: Duration typically available: Specific activity assigned: What makes this window unavailable on bad days:

Window 3: Time and trigger: Duration typically available: Specific activity assigned: What makes this window unavailable on bad days:

Add additional windows as identified.

What micro-recovery feels like for me (describe the state you are aiming for, not a standard description):

Section 2: Meso-Recovery Schedule

The meso-recovery session is thirty to sixty minutes, scheduled at the same time on the same days each week.

Session 1: Day and time: Duration: Activity or activities used: Person responsible for household during this session: What this session must not be conditional on:

Session 2 (if applicable): Day and time: Duration: Activity or activities used: Person responsible for household during this session: What this session must not be conditional on:

Conditionality list (list the things this session might be made conditional on, and confirm that none of them apply):

The meso-recovery session happens regardless of:

Section 3: Macro-Recovery Plan

The macro-recovery plan is for days or extended periods of substantially reduced demand load. Complete this section during a non-acute period.

Primary macro-recovery contact: Name: Contact: Specific responsibilities they cover during macro-recovery:

Secondary macro-recovery contact: Name: Contact: Specific responsibilities they cover during macro-recovery:

Minimum viable household definition (from Appendix B, summarised for this person's reference): What has to happen: What can drop: What the child needs that is non-negotiable:

Trigger for activating macro-recovery (the specific signal or score that initiates this plan):

Note to self for the macro-recovery period:

Write this during a non-acute period. Read it during the acute period when the self-critical loop says you should be managing better.

Section 4: Early Warning Indicators

Record the specific signals from Chapters 2.0 and 4.0 that appear first for you, in the sequence they typically appear. These are your personal early warning indicators, not the generic list.

First indicators (appear within the first week of depletion accumulating):

Second indicators (appear in the second to third week):

Cascade indicators (appear when burnout has progressed significantly):

When I see [first indicators], my response is:

When I see [second indicators], my response is:

When I see [cascade indicators], my response is:

Weekly Implementation Tracker

Week of: ____

Micro-recovery: window 1 completed (Y/N): ____ window 2: ____ window 3: ____

Meso-recovery: session 1 completed (Y/N): ____ session 2: ____

Obligation list review completed this week (Y/N): ____

Burnout early warning check completed (Y/N): ____

Notes on this week:

Appendix D Burnout Early Warning Signs Tracker

Instructions

This tracker is designed for daily use. It takes under two minutes per day. Complete it at the same time each day (many parents find it easiest immediately after the school drop-off, or at the end of the child's bedtime routine). Rate each item as 0 (not present), 1 (mild, noticeable but manageable), or 2 (significant, affecting function).

The threshold guide is at the end of this appendix. Do not use the threshold guide until you have at least five consecutive days of data.

Daily Tracking Grid

Signal / Day 1 / Day 2 / Day 3 / Day 4 / Day 5 / Day 6 / Day 7

Autistic Burnout Signals

1. Jaw tension (score 0-2)
2. Sound sensitivity above usual baseline (0-2)
3. Social masking felt harder than usual (0-2)
4. Preference for withdrawal or shutdown (0-2)

ADHD Depletion Signals 5. Task initiation difficulty (0-2) 6. Emotional response faster or more intense than usual (0-2) 7. Working memory gaps mid-task (0-2) 8. Decision fatigue earlier in day than usual (0-2)

PDA Parenting Exhaustion Signals 9. Co-regulation felt depleting rather than neutral (0-2) 10. Anticipatory parenting load high (0-2) 11. Repair capacity felt unavailable after difficulty (0-2)

Physical Signals 12. Sleep quality below usual baseline (0-2)

Daily Total (max 24):

Weekly Total:

Threshold Guide

Green (daily total 0-6, weekly total 0-28): Within sustainable range. Continue monitoring.

Amber (daily total 7-13 on two or more consecutive days, or any single day above 14): Early depletion signal. Review the micro-recovery map. Identify the highest-scoring layer. Apply targeted restoration for that layer. Increase monitoring frequency to twice daily for the following week.

Red (daily total above 14 on two or more consecutive days, or weekly total above 50, or three or more signals rated 2 on the same day for three consecutive days): Significant depletion. Apply the Chapter 5.0 audit immediately. Activate the meso-recovery schedule with full protection. If macro-recovery support exists, begin the activation process.

Pattern Notes

After four weeks of tracking, note: The signals that appear first for me: The signals that are most reliably present when I am most depleted: The specific time of day when signals are consistently highest: The days of the week when signals are consistently highest:

These patterns form your personal early warning profile.

Appendix E Support Network Mapping Tool

Instructions

Complete this tool during a period of relative stability rather than during an acute burnout. Honest assessment requires some distance from the acute state. Return to it and revise it as your support network changes.

Step 1: Current Network Inventory

List every person who currently provides, or who you believe provides, some form of support to you. Include professional support (therapist, GP, other practitioners), personal support (partner, family, friends), community support (parent groups, online communities), and practical support (anyone who provides operational help).

Name / Type of support / How frequently do you have contact

Step 2: The Support Audit

For each person listed, answer the three audit questions honestly.

After contact with this person, do I typically feel (circle one): Better / The same / Worse

Does the support they offer work in my actual household? (circle one): Yes / Partly / No

Does contact with this person require me to manage their emotional response? (circle one): Rarely / Sometimes / Usually

Scoring: Better + Yes + Rarely = high-quality support. Any other combination requires honest assessment of whether this relationship is primarily providing support or primarily requiring management.

Step 3: Minimum Viable Support Network

The minimum viable support network requires at least one person or source in each of the following three functions. Identify who currently fills each function, and where there are gaps.

Practical operational support (takes on specific recurring tasks or responsibilities without requiring initiation): Currently: Gap:

Emotional witness (can receive an honest account of my experience without reframing, advising, or requiring management of their response): Currently: Gap:

Professional support with framework compatibility (understands AuDHD and PDA; adapts approach to my executive function profile): Currently: Gap:

Step 4: Communication Scripts

Use these scripts as starting points. Adapt them to your specific relationships and communication style.

Script for communicating a burnout-related need to a practical support person:

"I am going through a difficult period at the moment and I am not managing well. The most useful thing right now would be [specific practical task]. Would you be able to [specific ask]? I do not need to talk about it, I just need the practical help."

Script for communicating a burnout-related need when you do not know specifically what you need:

"I am not managing well at the moment. I need support but I am not sure what form would help most. If you are able to offer something practical that I do not have to manage or explain, that would be the most useful. I will let you know when I have a clearer sense of what would help."

Script for communicating reduced capacity to someone with current expectations of you:

"I am not able to continue with [specific commitment] for the time being. I am dealing with a health situation that requires me to reduce my commitments. I will let you know when that changes. Thank you for understanding."

Script for telling a practitioner what you need from professional support:

"I am looking for a practitioner who has experience with AuDHD in adults and is familiar with PDA in children. I need an approach that can adapt to periods when my executive function makes standard homework assignments unfeasible. I am not looking for a practitioner who will recommend strategies that assume a neurotypical household. Can you tell me about your experience with this profile?"

Appendix F The Repair Conversation Guide

What Repair Is and Is Not

Repair in the relational sense is the process of restoring connection after a difficult interaction. It is not an apology that promises better future performance. It is not an explanation of the burnout and its neurological basis. It is not a therapeutic conversation that requires both people to be regulated and engaged. Repair, as used in this guide, is the minimum viable act of relational restoration: the signal sent by the parent to the child that the relationship is intact despite what happened.

For the AuDHD parent in burnout, this definition of repair is specifically important because it removes the expectation of full recovery before repair can begin. Repair does not require the parent to be at their best. It requires the parent to be present and non-hostile, and to communicate clearly that the relationship continues.

The Four Components of Minimum Viable Repair

Component 1: Timing. Repair does not happen during or immediately after a difficult interaction. Both nervous systems need a settling period first. For the PDA child, attempting repair while their threat-detection system is still activated is more likely to extend the dysregulation than to resolve it. Wait until both parent and child have settled, even partially.

Component 2: Brevity. Longer repair conversations are not more effective repair conversations. For the PDA child, a shorter repair is usually better received than a longer one because shorter conversations carry less demand. The repair does not need to cover everything. It needs to send the relational continuity signal.

Component 3: Honesty without detail. The repair acknowledges what happened honestly without requiring the child to process clinical detail. "That was hard" is honest. "I was in sensory overload because of my autistic burnout which is caused by the structural mismatch between my neurodevelopmental profile and the environmental demands" is accurate but not a repair conversation.

Component 4: Forward orientation. The repair ends with the relational continuity signal rather than the content of the difficulty. The ending point is the relationship, not the incident.

Age-Appropriate Repair Language

For children aged approximately 5 to 8:

"That was a hard time earlier. I was not at my best and I am sorry it felt bad. I love you and I am still here. Are you okay?"

For children aged approximately 9 to 13:

"Earlier was difficult. I was really depleted and I did not handle it well. That was not okay and it was not about you. Can we just sit for a bit?"

For teenagers:

"I want to acknowledge that earlier did not go well. I was running on empty and I handled it badly. That is not an excuse, it is an explanation. I am still here and I still want us to be okay. I do not need you to respond to that right now."

For the PDA child specifically, the repair language benefits from being lower demand than standard repair language. This means: no questions that require a response, no expectation of acknowledgement or forgiveness, no implied obligation for the child to reassure the parent. The repair is an offer, not an exchange.

PDA-adjusted versions:

Instead of "Are you okay?" (requires response): "I just wanted to let you know we are okay."

Instead of "Can we talk?" (demand): "I am around if you want to."

Instead of "I am sorry, will you forgive me?" (requires response): "I am sorry that was hard. I love you."

The Repair That Does Not Require Words

For some PDA children, particularly in the immediate aftermath of a difficult interaction, verbal repair is itself too high a demand. The non-verbal repair is the physical or environmental signal that communicates relational continuity without requiring any response: placing a preferred snack where the child will find it without comment, sitting in the same room doing something quiet, resuming a shared activity from before the difficult interaction without referencing what happened.

The non-verbal repair is not avoidance of repair. It is calibration of the repair to what the child's current nervous system can receive. A non-verbal repair that the child's nervous system can register is more effective than a verbal repair that the child cannot receive in their current state.

Repair After Extended Difficult Periods

When the burnout has produced an extended period of reduced parenting quality, the repair framework changes. Single incident repair is not adequate for extended difficult periods. What is needed is the gradual rebuilding of relational safety through repeated small consistent positive interactions over time, rather than a single significant repair conversation.

The minimum viable relational interaction from Chapter 9.0 is the tool for this rebuilding: the brief, daily, non-demanding shared moment that communicates the parent's continued presence and interest without requiring the child to engage at a level their nervous system cannot currently sustain.

Record your minimum viable relational interaction here:

Activity or moment: Time of day: Duration: What makes it low-demand for both of us: What makes it consistent and predictable for my child:

This interaction is not conditional on: (list the conditions that it might otherwise be made conditional on, and confirm none apply)

A Note on Your Own Repair

The repair this guide describes is between parent and child. There is also repair needed between the parent and themselves: the acknowledgement that the burnout produced parenting that fell below what the parent wanted to provide, and the self-compassionate response to that acknowledgement.

The self-repair does not require the parent to have fully recovered. It requires the same components as the parent-child repair: honesty without detail, brevity, and forward orientation. A note written to yourself, not requiring a response, not carrying the obligation of improvement, simply acknowledging what was hard and confirming that you are still here.

What would you say to a close friend who had been through what you have been through?

Write that here, directed at yourself.

That is the repair you also need.

Barkley, R. A. (1997). Behavioral inhibition, sustained attention, and executive functions: Constructing a unifying theory of ADHD. *Psychological Bulletin, 121*(1), 65–94.

Barkley, R. A. (2012). *Executive functions: What they are, how they work, and why they evolved.* Guilford Press.

Cage, E., & Troxell-Whitman, Z. (2019). Understanding the reasons, contexts and costs of camouflaging for autistic adults. *Journal of Autism and Developmental Disorders, 49*(5), 1899–1911.

Crompton, C. J., Ropar, D., Evans-Williams, C. V. M., Flynn, E. G., & Fletcher-Watson, S. (2020). Autistic peer-to-peer information transfer is highly effective. *Autism*, 24(7), 1704–1712.

Corden, K., Brewer, R., & Cage, E. (2021). Personal identity after an autism diagnosis: Relationships with self-esteem, mental wellbeing, and diagnostic timing. *Frontiers in Psychology*, 12, 699335.

Crompton, C. J., Fotheringham, F., Cebula, K., Webber, C., Foley, S., & Fletcher-Watson, S. (2024). Neurodivergent-designed and neurodivergent-led peer support in school: A feasibility and acceptability study of the neurodivergent peer support toolkit (NEST). *Autism & Developmental Language Impairments*, 9.

Craig, A. D. (2003). Interoception: The sense of the physiological condition of the body. *Current Opinion in Neurobiology, 13*(4), 500–505.

Fotheringham, F., Cebula, K., Fletcher-Watson, S., Foley, S., & Crompton, C. J. (2023). Co-designing a neurodivergent student-led peer support programme for neurodivergent young people in mainstream high schools. *Autism & Developmental Language Impairments*, 8.

Hermelin, B. (2001). *Bright splinters of the mind: A personal story of research with autistic savants*. Jessica Kingsley Publishers.

Kessler, R. C., Adler, L., Barkley, R., Biederman, J., Conners, C. K., Demler, O., Faraone, S. V., Greenhill, L. L., Howes, M. J., Secnik, K., Spencer, T., Ustun, T. B., Walters, E. E., & Zaslavsky, A. M. (2006). The prevalence and correlates of adult ADHD in the United States: Results from the National Comorbidity Survey Replication. *American Journal of Psychiatry, 163*(4), 716–723. (

Leedham, A., Thompson, A. R., Smith, R., & Freeth, M. (2020). 'I was exhausted trying to figure it out': The experiences of females receiving an autism diagnosis in middle to late adulthood. *Autism, 24*(1), 135–146.

Milton, D. E. M. (2012). On the ontological status of autism: The 'double empathy problem'. *Disability & Society, 27*(6), 883–887.

Neff, K. D. (2011). *Self-compassion: The proven power of being kind to yourself*. William Morrow.

Parham, L. D., Ecker, C., Kuhaneck, H. M., Henry, D. A., & Glennon, T. J. (2007). *Sensory Processing Measure (SPM): Manual*. Western Psychological Services.

Pearson, A., & Rose, K. (2021). A conceptual analysis of autistic masking: Understanding the narrative of stigma and the illusion of choice. *Autism in Adulthood, 3*(1), 52–60.

Porges, S. W. (2011). *The polyvagal theory: Neurophysiological foundations of emotions, attachment, communication, and self-regulation*. W. W. Norton & Company.

Raymaker, D. M., Teo, A. R., Steckler, N. A., Lentz, B., Scharer, M., Delos Santos, A., Kapp, S. K., Hunter, M., Joyce, A., & Nicolaidis, C. (2020). "Having all of your internal resources exhausted beyond measure and being left with no clean-up crew": Defining autistic burnout. *Autism in Adulthood, 2*(2), 132–143.

Schmitt, M. J., Neumann, R., & Montada, L. (1995). Dispositional sensitivity to befallen injustice. *Social Justice Research, 8*(4), 385–407.

Segerstrom, S. C., & Miller, G. E. (2004). Psychological stress and the human immune system: A meta-analytic study of 30 years of inquiry. *Psychological Bulletin, 130*(4), 601–630.

Shaw, P., Stringaris, A., Nigg, J., & Leibenluft, E. (2014). Emotion dysregulation in attention deficit hyperactivity disorder. *American Journal of Psychiatry, 171*(3), 276–293.

Siegel, D. J. (2012). *The developing mind: How relationships and the brain interact to shape who we are* (2nd ed.). Guilford Press.

Siegel, D. J., & Hartzell, M. (2003). *Parenting from the inside out: How a deeper self-understanding can help you raise children who thrive.* Jeremy P. Tarcher.

Solanto, M. V. (2011). *Cognitive-behavioral therapy for adult ADHD: Targeting executive dysfunction.* Guilford Press.

van der Kolk, B. A. (2014). *The body keeps the score: Brain, mind, and body in the healing of trauma.* Viking.

Volkow, N. D., Wang, G.-J., Newcorn, J. H., Kollins, S. H., Wigal, T. L., Telang, F., Fowler, J. S., Goldstein, R. Z., Klein, N., Logan, J., Wong, C., & Swanson, J. M. (2011). Motivation deficit in ADHD is associated with dysfunction of the dopamine reward pathway. *Molecular Psychiatry, 16*(11), 1147–1154.

Yehuda, R., & Lehrner, A. (2018). Intergenerational transmission of trauma effects: Putative role of epigenetic mechanisms. *World Psychiatry, 17*(3), 243–257

Young, S., Bramham, J., Gray, K., & Rose, E. (2018). The experience of receiving a diagnosis and treatment of ADHD in adulthood: A qualitative study of clinically referred patients using interpretative phenomenological analysis. *Journal of Attention Disorders*, 22(12), 1071–1084.

9 781764 563758